Explore Britain's
◆
Country
Gardens
◆

Produced by AA Publishing

Explore Britain's
Country Gardens

by Michael Wright

Foreword by Dr Stefan Buczacki

For Wendela, without whose inspiration this would not have been written.

Copy Editor: Rebecca Snelling

Published by AA Publishing, a trading name of Automobile Association Developments Limited, whose registered office is Norfolk House, Priestley Road, Basingstoke, Hampshire RG24 9NY. Registered Number 1878835

A catalogue record for this book is available from the British Library.

ISBN h/b 0 749 50682 2
      s/b 0 749 50772 1
      Hunter 1 55650-592-2

This book was produced using QuarkXPress™, Aldus Freehand™, and MicrosoftWord™ on Apple Macintosh™ computers.

Colour origination by L.C. Repro and Sons Ltd, Aldermaston.

Printed and bound by Butler and Tanner Ltd, Frome and London.

The contents of this book are believed correct at the time of printing. Nevertheless, the Publishers cannot accept responsibility for errors or omissions, or for changes in details given.

Acknowledgements: The Automobile Association wishes to thank the following photographers, libraries and associations for their assistance in the preparation of this book:

AA PHOTO LIBRARY with contributions from F/Cover D.Forss, B/Cover C.Mellor, B/Cover & Spine A.Baker, 6/7 D.Forss, 10 A.Baker, 11 K.Paterson, 13 J.Beazley, 14/5, 15 N.Ray, 16, 17a,b A.Baker, 18, 19, 20, 21 N.Ray, 22, 23 W.Voysey, 26, 27, 28, 29a,b A.Baker, 30, 31a,b N.Ray, 32, 33a,b A.Baker, 34, 35 N.Ray, 36, 37a,b A.Baker, 42, 43 N.Ray, 44/5, 45 A.Baker, 46/7 N.Ray, 48, 49 R.Hayman, 50, 50/1, 53 N.Ray, 54, 55, 62, 63a,b A.Baker, 64, 65, 66, 67 M.Birkitt, 68/9 N.Ray, 69 N.Ray, 70, 71, 72, 73a,b, 74, 75a,b, 76/7, 77, 78, 78/9, 80, 81a,b D.Forss, 82, 83a,b M.Birkitt, 84/5, 85a,b W.Voysey, 88, 89a,b D.Forss, 90, 91 W.Voysey, 92a,b, 93 D.Forss, 96, 97a,b, 98, 99a,b W.Voysey, 100/1, 101, 102, 103, 104, 104/5 M.Birkitt, 106 P.Baker, 108, 109a,b M.Birkitt, 110, 111 C.Mellor, 114/5a,b M.Birkitt, 117 C.Mellor, 118, 119, 120, 121a,b M.Birkitt, 122, 123a,b C.Mellor, 124/5, 125 I.Burgum, 126, 127 A.Tryner, 128, 129a,b I.Burgum, 130/1, 131 A.Tryner, 132/3, 133 I.Burgum, 136, 137a,b C.Mellor, 138/9, 139 A.Tryner, 140, 141 E.Bowness, 142, 143 J.Beazley, 144, 145a,b E.Bowness, 146 J.Morrison, 148, 149, 150/1, 151 K.Paterson, 152/3, 153 J.Beazley, 154/5, 155, 156/7, 158, 159 R.Weir, COTTESBROOKE HALL 12 Cottesbrooke Hall, DEREK FORSS 86/7 Leonardslee Garden, HADDON HALL 107 Haddon Hall, DAVID LEE/THE NATIONAL TRUST 116 Knot Garden, Moseley Old Hall, LEONARDSLEE GARDEN 86 The Dell, Leonardslee Garden, MANNINGTON GARDENS & COUNTRYSIDE 112/3 Mannington Hall Gardens, THE NATIONAL TRUST 24 The Courts, 25a Lily Pond, 25b Looking towards Temple, 38 Hidcote Manor Garden, 39 The Topiary, 40 Hidcote Manor House, 41 Flowers, 94 Sissinghurst Castle Garden, 95 Flowers in trough, NEWBY HALL & GARDENS 147 Newby Hall, THE PRIORY, KEMERTON 134/5 The Priory, STOURTON HOUSE GARDEN 52/3 The Garden, TREBAH GARDEN TRUST 56 Trebah Garden, 57 Tree Ferns, TRESCO ABBEY GARDENS 58 Tresco Abbey Gardens, 59a King Protea, 59b ships figurehead, TREWITHEN ESTATES 60 Horse, 61 The Garden

CONTENTS

✳

Foreword by Dr Stefan Buczacki
6

Location map
8

Introduction: A Celebration of Country Gardens
10

FOREWORD

by Dr Stefan Buczacki

I confess to being fortunate. I probably see more of Britain's gardens in the course of a year than some people manage in a lifetime. This is a great privilege although it is also a responsibility as I am frequently asked to recommend my favourite garden in this or that part of the country. But of course to single out one or even a handful of gardens from the phenomenal gardening richness of these islands is impossible. When someone sets out to convey so personal a matter as a selection of gardens to visit, therefore, I always wonder how

genuine and honest a choice this can be. But clearly, when the chooser is someone with the gardening and writing pedigree of Michael Wright, I need have no concern.

This beautiful book is a marvel of careful and perceptive observation. There are even a few gardens in here that I don't know, but I can certainly vouch for the veracity of the descriptions of the many that I do. And I can only compliment the author on his choice. For these truly are country gardens (appropriate enough for the

former editor of *Country Life*), quintessentially British and conveying a real cross-section of our national horticultural wealth. Of course some of the great and famous inevitably are here: Hidcote in Gloucestershire, Sissinghurst in Kent and, I am delighted to see, the garden that probably comes closest to my favourite of all, Hestercombe in Somerset. But almost more importantly, Michael Wright has included many of the less-known, yet no less significant gems: Jenkyn Place and Spinners in Hampshire, the exquisite headquarters of John Brookes at Denmans in Sussex, the charming Dorothy Clive Garden in Staffordshire, even the remarkable Heligan Manor in Cornwall, currently being restored and a garden that I had the pleasure of bringing to the public's notice through television. In fact, I'm not at all sure that this isn't the selection that I might have made myself.

Above all, however, the book is true to its title in that it invites you to explore, not merely to stand back and watch. You are Michael Wright's companion as he takes you through his chosen gardens, pointing out the best plants and most interesting features; and the fine AA map then leads you on to the next port of call. Yes, this really is the gardening guide for anyone who thought they'd seen them all.

The rose season at its glorious height at Penshurst Place in Kent

EXPLORE BRITAIN'S
COUNTRY GARDENS
*
Location
Map

Crathes
Castle ●

House of
Pitmuies ●

Plants from
the Past ●

Herterton
House ●

□ NEWCASTLE

□ EDINBURGH

SCOTLAND

□ GLASGOW

Crarae
Gardens ●

Brodick Castle ●

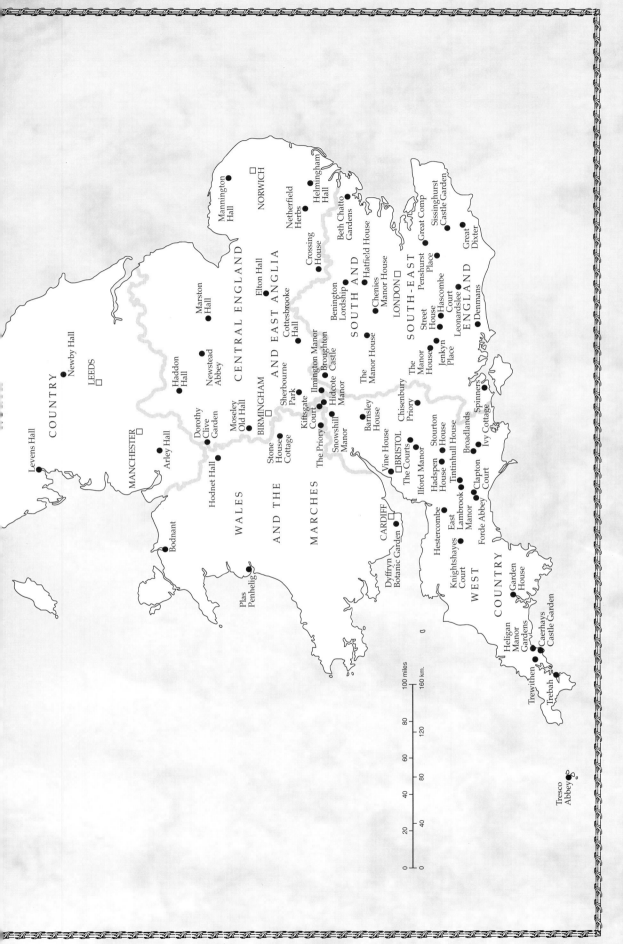

NORTH

Levens Hall

Newby Hall

LEEDS

NORTH
COUNTRY

MANCHESTER

Arley Hall

Marston
Hall

Haddon
Hall

Newstead
Abbey

Hodnet Hall

Bodnant

Plas
Penhelig

Dorothy
Clive
Garden

Moseley
Old Hall

BIRMINGHAM

CENTRAL ENGLAND

Elton Hall

Cottesbrooke
Hall

Sherbourne
Park

AND EAST ANGLIA

Mannington
Hall

NORWICH

Netherfield
Herbs

Helmingham
Hall

Crossing
House

Beth Chatto
Gardens

Benington
Lordship

Hatfield House

Kiftsgate
Court

Ilmington Manor

Broughton
Castle

Hidcote
Manor

The Priory

Snowshill
Manor

WALES
AND THE
MARCHES

Stone
House
Cottage

Vine House

Ilford Manor

DYFFRYN
Botanic Garden

CARDIFF

BRISTOL

The Courts

Barnsley
House

Chisenbury
Priory

Chenies
Manor House

The
Manor House

SOUTH AND

SOUTH-EAST

LONDON

Street
House

The
Manor
House

Penshurst
Place

Great Comp

Sissinghurst
Castle Garden

Great
Dixter

Hascombe
Court

Leonardslee

ENGLAND

Denmans

Jenkyn
Place

Hestercombe

Knightshayes
Court

Hadspen
House

Stourton
House

Tintinhull House

East
Lambrook
Manor

Clapton
Court

Forde Abbey

Broadlands

Ivy Cottage

Spinners

WEST COUNTRY

Garden
House

Heligan
Manor
Gardens

Caerhays
Castle Garden

Trewithen

Trebah

Tresco
Abbey

100 miles
160 km.

0   20   40   60   80   100
0   40   80   120   160

$\mathscr{A}$ CELEBRATION OF
COUNTRY GARDENS

*I*t is often said that when you scratch a British man or woman, you reveal a gardener. In planning and writing this book I soon came to understand the truth of this remark – not only in connection with the garden owners that I met, but also with regard to the many people for whom a summer would not be complete without tours of private gardens open in aid of the National Gardens Scheme, in the company of the wonderful 'Yellow Book', The Gardens of England and Wales, and the comparable book for Scotland. So many of us are beset every day by the noise and fumes of traffic and by the stress of urban living that country gardens become necessary oases of peace and beauty. We are all indebted to the owners for the diligence with which they trace the history of their gardens and explore others – for by their imagination, determination, enthusiasm and creativity, we can all be uplifted. And in practical terms, most garden visitors will take away with them, if not a plant to be treasured in what might prove to be a totally alien environment, at the very least an idea which will be adapted to their own surroundings. And thus even the most amateur of garden visitors plays a vital part in this seasonal orgy.

Choosing the gardens for inclusion in this book presented at least as many problems as the writing. Certainly, they had to be gardens with a strong individuality, either derived from the personality of their creator, or from the charm of the design and layout. Planting, too, had to be inspiring, with interesting flowers and – a modern requirement – striking foliage effects. Colour all the year round was also important, while on a more mundane level, I felt that the gardens described should be open to the public on a reasonable number of occasions during the year, as well as by appointment. (At the end of each article I have given a general indication of opening arrangements, but you are advised to check the details before making your visit.)

In selecting country gardens I wanted to concentrate on smaller gardens that were likely to be less familiar even to devoted garden visitors. In spite of my efforts, however, some great gardens – Hidcote Manor, the beautiful Sissinghurst, and Hestercombe amongst them – had to be included because of the influence that their designers have had on British gardening – not to mention the important impact that the gardens themselves have on all their visitors.

As visiting went on, it became steadily more apparent that there is a modern style of British country garden which derives from Lawrence Johnston's seminal layout at Hidcote Manor. The sense of enclosure, the surprise of unexpected vistas, and the distinct character of different parts of a garden are all elements of British gardening that we now take for granted. Just as important is the planting of a deep herbaceous border for visual effect, and here the gardeners have been influenced by that expert in colour harmony,

Left, midsummer at Hestercombe, Somerset

Below, the spacious lawns of Brodick Castle on the Isle of Arran

Gertrude Jekyll, who painted so skilfully with nature. Today, every gardener who places the hot reds and oranges in the middle of a border, reaching this crescendo of excitement from the cool colours of grey and blue at either end is, however unconsciously, in her debt.

Inevitably, in such a personal selection, some readers may be dissatisfied with what they will see as a regional imbalance in the choice of gardens, but it is unfortunately true that gardening is easier in the softer south and therefore many of the finest gardens are to be found in this part of the country. The regional differences of soil and climate make for rich variety in the gardens throughout Britain. Thus, to me, it is fascinating that the Gulf Stream makes it possible to grow tender plants so readily in Cornwall that they reach an amazing height and girth; and while I have included several gardens in that remarkable county, each is quite different from the others, and all are as famous for their role in the history of gardening as for their beauty today.

It has also proved entertaining to trace the hidden links of family, friendship and connoisseurship that connect so many of the gardens in this book. The names of the plant hunters George Forrest and E H Wilson appear again and again, and so do the hybridists J C Williams, Sir Edmund Loder and George Johnstone. They were responsible for fashions in plants at a particularly important time, so that many gardens in this book have fine examples of Magnolia campbellii and the Camellia williamsii hybrids. The story is not so different today, although the plants in vogue are more likely to be those with strong foliage contrasts, such as Lonicera nitida 'Baggesen's Gold', purple sage, Berberis thunbergii f. atropurpurea and Cotinus 'Royal Purple'.

No guide to gardens in this country could hope to be comprehensive, and I make no such claims for this one. Not only is the choice of garden a personal one, and the description of it inevitably seasonal as well as idiosyncratic, but the enthusiasms of the owner and of his or her gardener play an important part as well. I hope that this book is more than just a series of garden descriptions; perhaps it will open some readers' eyes, as it has opened mine, to new plants and their potentials; to using familiar plants in a novel way; and to fresh design ideas so obvious that they must surely have been germinating deep in one's own imagination. The objective must be to reawaken the most dormant of interest in plants.

MICHAEL WRIGHT

Left, a sunny courtyard garden outside Cottesbrooke Hall in
Northamptonshire

Above, the arcaded loggia of the Physic Garden at Herterton
House, Northumberland

BARNSLEY HOUSE
Gloucestershire
BARNSLEY, 4 MILES (6.5 KM) NORTH-EAST OF CIRENCESTER

Situated only 4 miles (6.5km) north of Cirencester, Barnsley is surely one of the prettiest stone villages in the Cotswolds. Like many a beauty, Barnsley House keeps its charms hidden until the last moment, but once the abrupt entrance drive has been negotiated the immediate and lasting impression is one of harmony. The honey-coloured Queen Anne house stands serenely amid 4 acres (1.6ha) of intimate garden enclosures interrupted by a sweeping lawn with softly coloured herbaceous borders.

Rosemary Verey and her late husband, David, began to design the garden in the 1960s and although the notion of natural growth is strongly evident, the bones of the garden are strong and maintenance is at a high level. On an axis from the drawing-room door a stone path, with its texture deliberately softened by clumps of geraniums and rock roses, runs straight to the centre of the south lawn which is flanked by generous plantings of aquilegias, stachys, phlomis and others in soft, muted colours. Beyond this, mature trees, including a purple sycamore, an atlas cedar and a silver-grey whitebeam, provide us with a marvellous contrast of foliage colours, textures and shapes.

Near to the house on the western side is a knot garden, with its little box hedges set in gravel in the manner of the formal parterres of the 16th and 17th centuries. The two squares of the knot have different designs, and a sundial surrounded by violas stands at the centre.

In the 1960s David Verey moved a temple dating from 1770 from Fairford Park to the south-east corner of the garden, thus creating a peaceful vista leading over the richly covered lily pond, through two iron gates flanked by statuesque cypresses, to a wall fountain at the other end.

Alongside Mrs Verey's potager, or decorative kitchen garden, runs a wonderful laburnum tunnel which in

Stone flower-girls flank the gateway leading to the vegetable garden

spring is thickly covered with yellow panicles reaching down to meet the tall, mauve alliums that rise from underneath.

This potager, inspired by the one at the Château de Villandry, in the Loire valley, is a truly remarkable creation. Brick paths in many different patterns criss-cross the area, and the beds themselves are planted with red and green varieties of lettuce and other vegetables, while sweetpeas grow close to gooseberries and onions, cabbages, lavender and strawberries. Perhaps the layout of the potager is typical of Barnsley House garden as a whole – a charming mixture of nonchalance and formality.

Open on selected days throughout the year. Tel: 0285 74281.

Barnsley House rises comfortably above a rich variety of foliage

BROADLANDS
Dorset

4 MILES (6.5 KM) SOUTH OF STURMINSTER NEWTON

Three different views of Broadlands, showing the rich variety of planting and structure in this attractive garden

Set in the rolling countryside of central Dorset, the gardens of Broadlands, at Hazelbury Bryan, skilfully conceal the fact that their full extent is only 2 acres (0.8ha). The design and planting of the garden has occupied the owners, Mr and Mrs M J Smith, for the past 17 years. Although no tricks of layout seem to be involved apart from the use of screening hedges, there are sudden views of the ornamental woodland and the vegetable garden, and the main lawn is broken up by island beds, creating a network of bays or small 'garden rooms' with an informal structure.

Much of the area in front of the vine-covered house is given over to lawn with three specimen trees – a variegated holly, a robinia with golden leaves and a Himalayan birch with a dramatic white trunk – while along the roadside hedges a shrub bed provides colour throughout the year. On the north side of the house grassy glades lead into a woodland area where fast-growing native and ornamental trees have been established and then underplanted with azaleas, rhododendrons, camellias and hydrangeas – all of which have now been underplanted in their turn by daffodils, hellebores and hostas.

The woodland is separated from a large lawn by a great beech hedge 120ft (36.5m) long and 8ft (2.4m) high.

Among the enclosed areas that break up the lawn is a cottage garden strikingly planted with geraniums, salvias, rock roses and echinops, together with other flowers chosen to give colour throughout the year. A recent development has been the creation of a large conservation pond and associated water garden, which adds greatly to the attractions of Broadlands. Now, colonies of frogs, toads, newts and dragonflies have settled the area, and wading birds also visit on occasions.

An archway gives access to a new rose garden featuring trellis and a curving pergola draped with climbing roses chosen for their fragrance as well as their colour, and with clematis contributing to the overall colour scheme of pink, white, crimson and silver. Shrub roses are naturalised in grass so that their fragrance can be appreciated at close quarters.

Broadlands is not only a charming country garden with appeal to the visitor at every season, it also has many unusual plants to intrigue the plant lover. It might even be described as an arboretum, as there are fine magnolias, viburnums, dogwoods and hollies, and, more important still, the plants are carefully labelled.

Open from June to August on selected days. Tel: 0258 817374.

CAERHAYS CASTLE GARDENS
Cornwall

GORRAN, 6 MILES (9.5 KM) SOUTH OF ST AUSTELL

The romantic castle at Caerhays is an early 19th-century creation of fantasy, and its garden is a rewarding voyage of discovery

On the south coast of Cornwall, close to the River Luney which reaches the sea in Porthluney Cove, is the vast and romantic Caerhays Castle. Built in the early years of the last century in the Gothick style by John Nash for John Bettesworth Trevanion, Caerhays came into the hands of the Williams family in 1853. It was John Charles Williams who created the gardens and financially supported the great plant hunters, E H Wilson and George Forrest. Today, still owned by the same family, Caerhays has an unrivalled collection of magnolias and shrubs which derive from this enterprise. J C Williams also specialised in the cultivation of daffodils, under the expert guidance of the Reverend Engleheart.

Leaving the west side of the castle, you approach the Auklandii Garden where, on the right, there are some great *Rhododendron arboreum* hybrids which are a century old, as well as an oak which was most probably sent to Caerhays from Louisiana by the great plant collector, Professor Sargent. Beyond the terrace, with its views of the house and the beach, the main path leads into the Tin Garden past some spectacular magnolias. The biggest of these is the *Magnolia Veitchii* 'Peter Veitch', which came from Veitch's great nursery in 1920, and a *Magnolia campbellii*, introduced to Britain in 1865. Rather curiously, its flowers appear before the leaves. Unfortunately the big storm of 1990 uprooted two large magnolias, each 80ft (24.3m) high. In this part of the garden there are both a fine rhododendron hybrid 'Crossbill' and a *Camellia reticulata* 'Captain Rawes', which is almost a century old.

To the right of the main route is Mr Roger's Quarry, where the best variety of *Magnolia campbellii* at Caerhays,

'November Pink', as well as azaleas and *Styrax japonica*, which produces white, bell-shaped flowers in early summer. Cornwall is a county rich in gardens and Caerhays is without doubt one of the most remarkable.

Open between March and May on selected days. Tel: 0872 501310.

Mollicamata 'Lanerth', which produces cyclamen purple flowers, can be seen. In addition to his work with rhododendrons, J C Williams crossed two species of camellia producing the *Camellia williamsii* hybrids which are seen extensively throughout the country today. A clump of one of the best varieties, 'J C Williams', which has single pink flowers in the late spring, is to be seen in the quarry.

Above the main path is a screen of laurel, a striking *Rhododendron sinogrande* and two hybrids raised at Caerhays, 'Emma Williams' and 'Veryan Bay'. The latter was one of the last hybrids cultivated by Williams. The steep path down from the Donkey Shoe past the Old Quarry to the castle gives a splendid view of one of the largest hybrid camellias in the garden,

Above, a delicate hydrangea in woodland setting.

CHISENBURY PRIORY
Wiltshire

6 MILES (9.5 KM) SOUTH-WEST OF PEWSEY

South of the Wiltshire town of Pewsey, the River Avon cuts a deep valley into the edge of Salisbury Plain. There, in deep countryside, stands Chisenbury Priory, a red-brick house – partly medieval but more predominantly Georgian – set in charming gardens of about 5 acres (2ha), created during the past 15 years by the owners, Mr and Mrs Alastair Robb.

In front of the house two deep, colourful borders frame the entrance court. Lady's mantle, catmint and sage stand in front of acanthus, artemisias and yellow achilleas, while wisteria and even a vine grow against the brick façade. Behind the house, well maintained lawns are flanked by striking brick walls topped with red tiles, and a laburnum tunnel with yew planted against its vertical posts curves across the upper garden. In cottage garden style, roses and clematis clothe the walls, while the tunnel path is bright with rock roses.

A flight of wide steps run through a border which separates the upper

A profusion of colour surrounds a rustic bench in the walled garden

A rampant clematis almost hides the wall

lawn from the lower, and here artemisias and lavender mix with red, pale pink and rose-coloured phlox. Specimen trees grow on the lawn which slopes gently down to a tributary of the Avon. Here, astilbes, hostas, lilies and gunnera enliven the water's edge, while over a flint-and-stone-bridge espaliered fruit trees mark the end of that part of the garden.

Beyond the wall, the character of the gardens undergoes another change, with an extensive wildflower meadow and another cottage border, dominated by hollyhocks underplanted with geraniums, against the wall.

Mrs Robb also has many rare South African plants at Chisenbury, some of which are tender and kept in pots so that they can be moved into the greenhouse during the winter. Many of the plants that the visitor will have admired during a tour of the garden are propagated here and can be bought, as can a light, white wine made from the Chisenbury vines. These little touches add much to a beautiful garden which, by its diversity of habitat and charming planting, already has much to commend it.

Open on selected days between May and September.

CLAPTON COURT
Somerset

CLAPTON, 3 MILES (5 KM) SOUTH OF CREWKERNE

To the south of Crewkerne the road to Lyme Regis plunges deep into the lush, well-wooded Somerset countryside, crossing the valley of the River Axe, and before long you come upon one of the most beautiful and varied gardens in a county which is rich in such hidden delights. Clapton Court consists of 4 acres (1.6ha) of formal gardens, an equal area of woodland, and a splendid nursery offering a wide range of unusual plants, many of which can be seen flourishing in their natural setting.

The bones of the formal garden were established by Louis Martineau over a period of 25 years from the late 1940s, with a series of low walls built on three terraces on a natural slope facing south-west. In 1978, when the garden had declined, Captain Simon Loder, the present owner and nephew of the creator of Leonardslee Garden

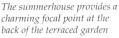

The summerhouse provides a charming focal point at the back of the terraced garden

in Sussex, bought Clapton Court and restored and greatly extended it, introducing many unusual shrubs and other plants.

Emerging from the nursery through a gate on to a gravel path that runs along the lower terrace to the left, the eye is drawn to one of the middle terraces stunningly planted with soft-silver colours in a formal box-edged layout. But one is encouraged to walk along past the lawn with mixed borders planted in shades of blue, white and pink. Laurel and yew hedges provide a backdrop to catmint, astrantia, rock roses and a striking *Euonymus fortunei*.

Higher up the path, the second terrace is laid out primarily with silver and white plants, including *Artemesia ludoviciana*, lavender and hostas, growing below four small standard salixes. Aubretia and campanulas tumble over the surrounding walls, and a seat, set into an alcove of clipped cypress, gives a beautiful vista past a fine weeping pear through an opening in the yew hedge. The view continues across a sundial in the next enclosure to the lily pond, behind which a curved wooden bench is surrounded by a semi-circular cypress hedge.

The top terrace is given over almost entirely to red and pink roses, while a yellow border, bright with *Syringa vulgaris* 'Primrose', euphorbias, santolinas, jasmine and lilies, leads to a charming summerhouse, backed by shady woodland. Beneath the shelter of oak and pines, seasonal colour is provided by camellias, azaleas, rhododendrons, hydrangeas, mahonia and geraniums, while in the larger woodland there is red sycamore, a ginkgo, magnolia, and Britain's largest ash, *Fraxinus excelsior* – over 200 years old, with a girth of 23 feet (9m). With the swathes of daffodils and other spring bulbs, Clapton Court is a garden of beauty and interest at all times of the year.

Open on most days, from March to October.

The lily pond, with a splendid autumnal chestnut tree behind

THE COURTS
Wiltshire

HOLT, 3 MILES (5 KM) SOUTH-WEST OF MELKSHAM

Although owned by the National Trust, the beautiful gardens of The Courts retain a sense of mystery, standing as they do behind high stone walls in the centre of the village of Holt. As its name suggests, The Courts was the building where the cloth weavers of Bradford-on-Avon, a mile away, brought their 1921, however, it was owned by Major T C E Goff and Lady Cecilie, his wife, and it was she who, influenced by Gertrude Jekyll, laid out the series of 'garden rooms' at The Courts which offer an ever-changing series of vistas and make the visitor feel that the gardens are bigger than their 7 acres (2.8ha).

Stone garden ornaments and a sturdy yew hedge echo the formal strength of the house in the background

disputes for settlement, and indeed at one time cloth was made on the site as a cloth mill stood next to the house. In 1900 the well-known architect, Sir George Hastings, bought The Courts, introduced many of the architectural features to its garden – including the yew and box hedges as a background for the stone ornaments – and built the conservatory. From

The garden is reached through an avenue of pleached limes at the front of the house. At the end of the lawn there is a fernery backed by a *Lonicera nitida* hedge. To the east of the house (which is not open to the public) is a lawn dominated by eight stone pillars that used to have chains hung between them for drying the cloth produced at the mill. Around the central stone

Roses, lavender and astilbes border the lily pond

feature is the silver *Anaphalis* 'Pearl Everlasting', and *Verbena* 'Sissinghurst', while the left-hand border is planted with penstemons, geraniums, irises, violas and *Centauria hypoleuca* 'John Coutts'. Opposite is a mainly herbaceous border bright with montbretia and berberis, while the bedding plants are modern cultivars of the annual rudbeckias.

The lily pond was made by Lady Cecilie Goff, and its paved area is dominated in autumn by sumach and a purple berberis underplanted with bergenias and diascias. The pond itself boasts dark-red, pink and white waterlilies, and is surrounded by a herbaceous bed planted with lavenders, irises and roses. The borders beyond the lily pond are full of hostas, astilbes, rodgersias, and a fragrant *Viburnum carlesii*.

A path runs around the natural shape of the lower pond to re-emerge in front of a stone pavilion where there are two deep borders planted with pink-, yellow- and purple-flowering perennials, including many hemerocallis. The Venetian Gate borders, which lead on to the house lawn, are edged with lilies, red hot pokers, lychnis and echinops. At the corner of the main lawn, to the west, is a grotto made of tufa, while a path behind it is edged with clumps of Japanese sacred bamboo and angel's fishing rod. At the end of the main lawn, the sundial is surrounded by artimesias, flag irises and two clipped, weeping pears, while the blue and yellow borders are rich with geraniums, euphorbias, achilleas and Michaelmas daisies.

Open on selected days, from April to October. Tel: 0225 782340.

Leafy borders lead up to the Temple

EAST LAMBROOK MANOR GARDEN
Somerset

2 MILES (3 KM) NORTH-EAST OF SOUTH PETHERTON

*B*oth in its size and in the style of its planting, East Lambrook Manor richly deserves the label of cottage garden. Although the garden which Margery and Walter Fish created here from 1938 only covers 2 acres (1ha), many of the traditional plants typical of the 19th-century cottage garden would have been lost to cultivation had they not been collected and planted here. To these were added some of the flowers popularised by Gertrude Jekyll in her rather grander layouts in the first three decades of this century. Today Mrs Fish's work is continued and renewed by Mr and Mrs Andrew Norton, and many of the unusual species that can be seen in the garden are available in the plant sales area. East Lambrook also houses the national collection of geraniums, that is cranesbill, as well as important groups of primulas, euphorbias and lavender.

When you enter this pretty garden through the orchard there are two quite small areas in front of you. To the left the Green Garden is set off by a medlar, a Judas tree and, appropriate for this part of the Somerset Levels, a Glastonbury thorn. Under this generous shade euphorbias, aquilegias, a white iris and begonias flourish. Contrasting with this 'garden room' is the Sundial Garden, where a Mexican orange, yellow potentillas and the wild geranium 'herb Robert' crowd around the sundial itself. The Knoll, which lies alongside the malthouse, centres on a black mulberry and is edged by hebes, helianthemums, yellow cistus and pink geraniums, while at the end of the lawn is a herb garden edged with honeysuckle and containing sages, lavender, purple basil, lovage and angelica.

Here you climb steps between sturdy *Chamaecyparis lawsonia* 'Fletcheri' to be greeted at the end of the avenue by a beautiful weeping pear with its bluey-silver leaves. Towards the south wall of the malthouse is a terrace planted with yellow lilies, scabious, cranesbill and red campion. The malthouse wall itself is covered with wisteria and red berberis. At the top of the path, the White Garden boasts the trunks of silver birches and the white, double clematis 'Duchess of Edinburgh', and a white climbing rose. In the adjoining Silver Garden are artemisias, *Stachys lanata* and lychnis. Beyond this first section of the garden is a paved circle with a border holding *Artemisia stelleriana* with almost white leaves, the feathery textured *discolor*, and *ludoviciana* with its lance-shaped leaves. This is not a garden to be missed by those who appreciate the cottage style, or the rare plants which, but for Mrs Fish's enterprise, might well have been lost for ever.

Open from March to October on selected days. Tel: 0460 40328.

Above, the garden at East Lambrook, designed around the old stone manor house, the malthouse (left) and the cowhouse, has been lovingly brought back to life

The herbaceous bed runs along the edge of the Long Pond

FORDE ABBEY
Dorset

4 MILES (6.5 KM) EAST OF CHARD

Close to the banks of the Axe, which marks the county boundary between Somerset and Dorset, are the splendid gardens of Forde Abbey. Occupied as a private house since 1649, the former Cistercian abbey buildings are set in a beautiful and varied garden. Bright borders are backed by honey-coloured stone walls, and wide sloping lawns are punctuated by mature trees, while a chain of ponds, once the monks' fish ponds, now feature cascades and are embellished with statuary.

Entering through the walled gardens where the excellent nursery is housed, around the side of the abbey, the first view leads up to a statue flanked by two yews at the end of two deep, immensely colourful flower borders. With the Long Pond running along the back of the left-hand herbaceous bed, the eye is drawn to the enormous variation of height and colour provided by the statuesque *Nicotiana sylvestris* jostling with shrub roses, hydrangeas and irises, underplanted with salvias, silver stachys, tradescants and many others. Beyond is the Mount, from the top of which you can enjoy a wonderful birds'-eye view back over the Long Pond and the cone-shaped, clipped yews on either side of the herbaceous borders. The Mount itself is dominated by trees, including a great redwood *Sequoia sempervirens* and the incense cedar, *Calocedrus decurrens*.

The path runs through parkland further to the north and, after tantalising views of the 4 acre (1.6ha) Great Pond, enters the bog garden created from an area of the pond that has been silted up for centuries. In this, one of the most beautiful areas of the gardens, you can see a wide range of variegated grasses, astilbes, the ruby-coloured lobelia, meconopsis, irises and, dotted around, masses of elegant candelabra primulas overhung by giant gunnera and rustling bamboo.

At the southern margin of the Great Pond is the remarkable Beech House. It is carved from growing tree trunks, and even has a window overlooking the lake. On the return journey towards the abbey buildings you pass an 18th-century ha-ha, a ditch dug to keep animals within the park without the view being interrupted by a fence. The rock garden was created out of an old gravel pit before World War I, and supports many interesting plants, including a *Hydrangea petiolaris* which climbs a thorn tree beside the top pool.

In an area that boasts many fine gardens, those at Forde Abbey stand out as being not only beautiful, but also notable for the many rare plants which have been laid out to complement the attractive stone of the abbey buildings.

Open daily, all year. Tel: 0460 21366.

Part of the water garden (below), and the magnificent rock garden

THE GARDEN HOUSE
Devon

BUCKLAND MONACHORUM, 5 MILES (8 KM) SOUTH OF TAVISTOCK

Above, the captivating walled garden with its deep borders

Right above, a carved stone doorway leading to the Garden House

Right below, an example of the delicate Campanula lactiflora

Situated on a hillside to the west of Dartmoor, the Garden House covers 7 acres (2.8ha) of a valley which runs down to the River Tavy. There are records of a vicarage at Buckland Monachorum in the 14th century, but the old tower with its spiral staircase, which is such a feature of the walled garden, dates from the 16th century when the abbot of the dissolved Buckland Abbey changed his religious affiliations to become the vicar. After 1945 the garden was the creation of Lionel Fortescue, a retired Eton classics master, and his wife, but today the garden is owned by a trust, and the planting is in the hands of Keith and Ros Wiley who have gardened at Buckland since 1978.

As you enter the walled garden from the plant sales centre, the impact of the long, grassed path flanked by deep, colourful borders is quite captivating. Astilbes, campanulas, lilies and the gentle pink of *Lavatera* 'Barnsley' are planted among old roses, including 'Golden Wings' and 'Dortmund'. At this lower level the soil is damp and hostas and the rheums flourish, while erythroniums, wood anemones and crocuses flower in the spring. A short flight of steps takes you down into a little dell where magnolias, roses and philadelphus add their distinctive scents.

Throughout the garden care has been taken to group trees and shrubs for the harmony and the contrast of

their foliage and flowers, so the red and the paler berberis can be seen, as can the purple of cotinus and the silver of willows and dogwoods, particularly the *Cornus controversa* 'Variegata', the 'wedding cake tree', with its white, star-shaped flowers. The exacting standards in colour harmony set by the garden's creators have been maintained today, so that a deep blue clematis is partnered by *Viburnum tomentosum*, with its lace-cap flowers and red fruits.

The tower staircase provides access to the second terrace. Here is the main lawn with a round stone seat formed like a lookout at the far end, its entrance guarded by two willows underplanted with cranesbill. There is also an alpine garden where miniature geraniums grow alongside silver plants, and on the very top terrace is a fine collection of rhododendrons, a willow-leaved magnolia, and a *Magnolia x loebneri* 'Leonard Messel', which has lilac-pink petals in mid-spring. This is a delightful place with rare plants – many of which can be bought in the nursery – that never loses the intimacy and individuality of a private garden.

Open daily, from April to September. Tel: 0822 254769.

HADSPEN HOUSE
Somerset

2 MILES (3 KM) SOUTH-EAST OF CASTLE CARY

Set in the lush Somerset countryside, Hadspen is a fine garden with a distinguished pedigree. The manor house was built of the golden Ham stone of the area by the Hobhouse family in the 18th century, but the basic structure of the garden was established by Margaret Hobhouse in the great days of British gardening at the end of the last century. After some decades of neglect, the well-known gardening writer and designer, Penelope Hobhouse, undertook restoration. The property is now owned by Mr Niall Hobhouse, and the garden and nursery are managed by Mr and Mrs Pope.

As the main garden is now separated from the house, which is not open to the public, the visitor enters at the highest point of a south-facing slope, where there is a splendid lily pond created by Penelope Hobhouse out of a large water tank. Here, in raised beds set in gravel, silver plants such as stachys, thyme and purple sage predominate. The old walled kitchen garden has been filled by Mr and Mrs Pope with shrubs and herbaceous plants rather than with vegetables, and a border with tall shrubs and climbers runs along a wall leading down into the valley. Hadspen holds the national collection of rodgersias, and in this shady dell you can see some of the best varieties, including *R. pinnata* 'Superba' and *R. sambucifolia*. Near by, a double border is protected by beech hedges which were planted specifically to create good conditions for the extensive collection of hostas, including the cultivars 'Hadspen Blue' and 'Hadspen Heron'.

Beyond a bisecting gravel path edged with catmint, the borders are planted with yellow-flowering herbaceous plants – yellow lupins, roses and hypericum, Jerusalem sage and rock roses. Just as striking, with its silver- and grey-leaved plants, is the border which faces the kitchen garden. Senecios, santolinas and artemisias contrast with a morning glory bush and with eleagnus.

You can follow the bamboo path past the Victorian summerhouse to a small pond, then continue up alongside Victorian shrubberies, past a meadow area which supports fritillaries in spring and orchids in early summer, to a late 19th-century fountain where an earlier Hobhouse

laid out a terrace in the Italian style with ornate stone-work and beds for annuals. As would be expected at a garden of the quality of Hadspen, changes are continually being made, and many plants not otherwise readily found can be purchased in the nursery.

Open from March to October on selected days. Tel: 0963 50939.

Left and top, the gardens at Hadspen show a wide variety of planting, including the sprawling catmint borders (above), backed with white roses

HELIGAN MANOR GARDENS
Cornwall

PENTEWAN, 4 MILES (6.5 KM) SOUTH OF ST AUSTELL

A delicate 'lacecap' hydrangea

The work that is going on at Heligan, to the south of Mevagissey (and which will most probably continue for some years to come) is nothing less than the rediscovery of a lost garden. Heligan Manor was the home of the Tremayne family for centuries before World War I, and the 57 acres (23ha) of gardens that almost totally surrounded the house were regarded by many as one of the finest Victorian romantic layouts in the country.

The house itself was made into flats 20 years ago, but Tim Smit and his wife, Candy, formed a company to undertake restoration of the gardens and are doing so with much local

Tree ferns in the Jungle Garden, untouched for some 70 years

goodwill, and financial and practical assistance from all sides, as well as grants from the Countryside Commission.

Walking south along the Ride, you soon come to the Ravine. This was clearly a man-made rockery, using imported stone, which stretched for more than 100yds, and originally contained a collection of alpines. The water system for The Ravine was supported by three pumps set in a corbelled chamber 18ft (5.4m) below the ground, and this raised water to a large reservoir serving both the garden and the house. Remarkable as it might seem, the invoice for installing the system at Heligan in 1880 has recently come to light, and it now seems likely that the pipes can be traced and restored to working order. Even the old paths have been located with the help of a 1839 Tithe Map, and the loam and ivy which covered them for more than 80 years have been peeled back to reveal the surface and the land drains in good condition.

On Flora's Green, to the east of the Ride, is a fine group of rhododendrons, many of them collected by Sir Joseph Hooker in Sikkim and Bhutan, and planted at Heligan in the 1850s. Near by is a splendid *Magnolia campbellii*, and also a *Cornus capitata* 'Bentham's cornel', which has pale yellow bracts in early summer followed by red fruits in autumn.

Below the Northern Summerhouse, with its spectacular views over St Austell Bay, is the Dell. This boasts a collection of New Zealand plants, as well as tree ferns, which are thought to have been imported by the Tresidder family of Truro in the 1890s as ballast in their boats.

As one would expect of a Victorian garden, there is also a man-made grotto. It is lined with crystal and set amid a shady rockery with a wishing well. Towards the house is a wall with vaulted cells for holding bees, which most probably dates from the 1850s, while the flower garden, with its 300ft (91m) herbaceous border, is the next priority in this amazing programme of restoration.

Open daily throughout the year.

HESTERCOMBE HOUSE GARDENS
Somerset

CHEDDON FITZPAINE, 2 MILES (3 KM) NORTH-EAST OF TAUNTON

Lutyens' elegant orangery gives a focus to the garden

Set high on a south-facing slope overlooking the valley of the River Tone, with distant views of the Blackdown Hills in Somerset, are the gardens of Hestercombe House. They are one of the best surviving examples of the collaboration between Sir Edwin Lutyens and Gertrude Jekyll, built for the Hon E W B Portman between 1903 and 1908, and now owned and maintained with sensitivity by Somerset County Council as the headquarters for the county fire service.

The gaunt house and upper terrace were already in existence when Lutyens came to Hestercombe, and the dynamic of his design was to concentrate the garden interest to the south, fully engaging the magnificent views over the surrounding countryside. By the use of a classical open-air rotunda, he changed the direction of the 19th-century terrace to include a baroque orangery of great elegance, which he himself designed, and a Dutch garden. Lutyens used local materials, such as Morte slate from behind the house, and golden limestone from Ham Hill near Yeovil, and introduced flights of circular steps to create spaciousness. Water, too, was used to create tranquillity, and rills run from recessed ponds – to the west through a rose garden, and to the east from the rotunda pool.

From quite early on in her career Miss Jekyll was extremely myopic, and her planting at Hestercombe and elsewhere was concerned with the texture, overall shape and perfume of plants, as well as with their colour. The

Grey Walk, below the upper terrace, is planted throughout in soft colours. Greys, silver, mauve and white predominate, with lavender, rosemary and pinks interplanted with catmint, while strongly scented choisyas are used at the end of the border, and yuccas and blue thistles give structure to the overall composition.

The central area has a formal layout with beds filled with pink roses that contrast sharply with the strong leaves of the surrounding *Bergenia cordifolia*.

Peonies, lilies and delphiniums catch the eye, and a pergola overhung with climbing roses, honeysuckle and clematis creates a fragrant as well as a colourful and shady path in summer. Characteristic of Lutyens's attention to detail are the circular windows cut in the south walls of the pergola, and the alternately square and circular pillars that hold up the cross-beams of the structure.

Open on selected days throughout the year. Tel: 0823 337222.

Below left, roses and clematis intertwine above the pathway

Below, detail of a bearded waterspout

HIDCOTE MANOR GARDEN
Gloucestershire

4 MILES (6.5 KM) NORTH-EAST OF CHIPPING CAMPDEN

One of the most beautiful of English gardens, Hidcote Manor is the creation of one remarkable man, Major Lawrence Johnston. Born in Paris of American parents, Johnston grew up in France, and one can see in the formal arrangement of the series of outdoor 'rooms' in the garden the influence, perhaps, of Le Nôtre, as well as of his own architectural training.

Certainly he inherited what was virtually an empty site in 1907, with the exception of a clump of beeches and a fine cedar. His instincts for formality, however, were overlaid both by his wish to re-create the beauties of the traditional cottage garden so evocatively captured in the paintings of Helen Allingham, and by his plant-hunting expeditions to South Africa in 1927 with Major Collingwood Ingram, and in 1931 to Yunnan in China with George Forrest.

Lawrence Johnston's ideas have so often been copied that it is hard to imagine what a novel conception Hidcote must have been in 1914. The tapestry colours of the mixed holly, yew, box and beech hedge around the Fuchsia Garden, the copper beech and hornbeam hedge enclosing the Circle, the different textures of the yew and the holly alongside each other, and the tall, clipped yew hedges surrounding the Theatre Lawn, are now accepted style. But how remarkable they must have been at the time, and what diversity they give to Hidcote today.

The main axis of the garden runs

Left, a profusion of greenery, and below, the more formal White Garden at Hidcote

Lawrence Johnston was influenced by the paintings of Helen Allingham, as may be observed from this riot of sweet peas before the house

from the original cedar of Lebanon, which shades the Old Garden, through the Cottage Borders, the Circle and the Red Borders, and into the Stilt Garden. This formal composition lies alongside the Theatre Lawn, bordered by yew and featuring a raised, circular grass stage crowned by an old beech. The Stilt Garden can be approached through a gap in the yew hedge, and consists of double rows of pleached hornbeams which join at both ends. Through a little brick pavilion you can see the Long Walk running away at right angles, cunningly crossing a little stream as it makes its way to the southern boundary of the garden.

The Red Borders are boldly planted with dark-red cherries, cannas and hemerocallis, while the borders in front of the house are filled with flowers in the Allingham manner, but with the skilful colour harmony associated with Gertrude Jekyll. The central border is pink and mauve with campanula 'Hidcote Amethyst', a purple hibiscus, irises and potentillas, phloxes and peonies, while the northern border is mainly blue and white, and includes clematis, abutilon, philadelphus and the yellow climbing rose, 'Lawrence Johnston'. In the south border there are rhododendrons and the white pendulous *Magnolia sinensis*, as well as poppies and hydrangeas climbing over the walls.

The view from the Circle through the Fuchsia Garden, with its colourful beds surrounded by low box hedges, is one of Hidcote's most striking compositions. The Bathing Pool, despite its name, was designed purely for its visual effect and the circular pond is provided with a stone surround for sitting on, while a magnolia, the rose 'Fruhlingsgold' and drooping sedges are given an additional drama by the surrounding dark-green yew hedges. Many of the plants in the lush Stream Garden come from China, Tibet and Japan, including unusual varieties of camellia and rhododendron, as well as bog arums, giant lilies and *Gunnera manicata*. In

Mrs Winthrop's Garden, designed by Johnston for his mother, the theme is yellow with lilies, peonies, golden lysimachia and *Lonicera nitida* 'Baggesen's Gold'. The Pillar Garden, too, is filled with peonies, and contrast is provided in spring by the magnolias, and in summer by alliums and lilac.

Much of the charm of Hidcote derives from the contrast between formal layout and subtle planting. The colour harmony of the beds and the setting of the stone house in the midst of wonderful Gloucestershire countryside is guaranteed to bring the visitor back to the garden again and again.

Open from April to October, on selected days . Tel: 0386 438333.

A border rich in red flowers and foliage leads to steps and an inviting open gate

*The Casita – a perfect
harmony of plants, light and
stonework*

IFORD MANOR GARDENS
Wiltshire

2½ MILES (4 KM) SOUTH-WEST OF BRADFORD-ON-AVON

Occupying a steep hillside above the languorous River Frome, the fascinating gardens of Iford Manor are a subtle blend of Italianate layout and English planting. This was the garden created by the distinguished architect and landscape designer, Harold Peto – a partner of the turn-of-the-century country house architect, Ernest George, and a great influence on his young assistant, Edwin Lutyens. The topography of Iford lent itself to the strong architectural framework of terraces, and the predominant theme of the design is Italian, with plantings of cypress, juniper, box and yew interspersed with stone sarcophagi, urns, marble seats and statues, columns and loggias. The whole is presented with stunning light and shade effects that are almost theatrical.

The garden is entered by a loggia at the south-east corner of the Tudor house. Across the paved courtyard is a semi-circular pond, and Peto set an Italian Renaissance window (with its original glass) into the loggia, while the balconies above are wrought iron, dating from 1450. Worn steps lead up to the second terrace and the conservatory where two ancient fluted columns stand. Below the flight of steps that takes you up to the lawn are a pair of Italian marble lions dating from 1200. Here the planting complements the grey stone, with wisteria and other climbing plants and purple sage predominating. Brighter colours are also in evidence, with the pink of escallonias, red roses, gladioli

small 18th-century tea-house at the other, with senecio rambling over the paving and rosemary growing in the middle of a millstone. The Casita has pink marble columns, a dancing nymph in the inside niche, and a 14th- century Venetian Gothic wheel window, while its courtyard is planted with lavender, artemisias and rosemary. On the south side of the terrace a bronze wolf suckles Romulus and Remus, and the bed below the statue

and cotinus catching the eye, and with the Chilean glory flower growing on the steps. Peto created a small pool at this level, planted with potentillas, while shallow steps lead to a paved area overflowing with lady's mantle and punctuated by day lilies, shaded by a weeping birch. The Blue Pool has a Romanesque bas relief depicting a woman riding a lion set into the wall, and the pool itself is surrounded by honeysuckle and pink roses.

The Great Terrace runs from a curved seat at its western end to a

contains irises, berberis and meadow rue. In the woodland to the north, the owners, Mr and Mrs Cartwright-Hignett, are constructing a Japanese water garden begun by Harold Peto, and beyond the Roman sarcophagus is an 18th-century tea-house. Through a charming arbour of berberis, beeches and laburnum are the cloisters, built by Peto in the Italian Romanesque style to house antique fragments.

Open from April to October, on selected days. Tel: 02216 2364.

Italian urns stand along the Great Terrace

IVY COTTAGE
Dorset

ANSTY, 12 MILES (19 KM) NORTH OF DORCHESTER

*A*nsty stands in that open rolling country to the west of Blandford Forum which is so typical of Dorset. Chalk underlies most of the area, and the enchanting gardens of Ivy Cottage, in Aller Lane, lie on greensand. Springs abound, while a little stream flows out of woodland and across the edge of the lawn, ensuring that, even in the driest weather, the plants are always well watered. This is an ideal habitat for primulas, irises and gunneras, and in particular for trollius and the moisture-loving lobelias, for which Ivy Cottage holds the national collections.

In front of the thatched cottage large herbaceous borders on either side of the main lawn slope down towards the lane. Perennial ajugas form a dense foliage carpet at the front of the bed, with pulmonarias, irises

The stream ensures that this cottage garden does not dry out in the summer

and several varieties of hostas. In the middle of the border stands *Euphorbia polychroma*, geraniums, *Stachys macrantha* and several varieties of oriental poppy, while day lilies provide bright colour in the summer. Conscious of the need to give year-round colour, the owner, Mrs Anne Stevens, has planted echinops, aruncus and lychnis at the back of the border, with Michaelmas daisies, Japanese anemones and *Salvia involucrata* 'Bethellii' taking over in the autumn. Between the plants are bulbs of all kinds – snowdrops, crocus and narcissi in the spring, alliums in the summer.

Beyond the borders you pass a young cedar, which has been underplanted with cyclamen and crocus, to reach a new bed standing in the shade of birches and a handkerchief tree. Here the soil is slightly acid, and young camellias and enkianthus are backed by the purple-leaved elders and Asiatic primulas. A small wooden bridge crosses the stream and leads to the kitchen garden where flowers as well as vegetables, surrounded by hedges of parsley and marigolds, are grown. Near the kitchen garden is a large triangular bed filled with moisture-loving plants such as candelabra primulas, astilbes, trollius and *Rodgersia podophylla*.

A grassy path winds through woodland where ash and poplar shade azaleas and rhododendrons, and where primroses and marsh marigolds give a wonderful display in the spring. Behind the cottage, the damp bank of

the Ditch Garden supports irises and *Ligularia przewalskii* 'The Rocket', with yellow flowers on a dark brown stem, lysichiton, and an extremely large gunnera. To the right of the drive the ground is much drier, and in the border backed by a high beech hedge there are penstemons, salvias and alliums. This is undoubtedly a wonderful cottage garden, maintained to the highest standards and supporting many unusual plants.

Open from April to October, on selected days. Tel: 0258 880053.

A vision of England – the perfect thatched cottage in the perfect cottage garden

Situated high up in the Cotswold Hills above the Vale of Evesham, Kiftsgate has natural advantages of topography which, in the past, have been enhanced by its proximity to the great garden of Hidcote (see page 38). It is, perhaps, rare to find two such fine gardens so close together, but Heather Muir, who built the Kiftsgate gardens from 1920, was a close friend of Lawrence Johnston, the creator of Hidcote, and Kiftsgate undoubtedly benefited from Major Johnston's plant-hunting expeditions to Japan and China. Today, the gardens are beautifully maintained by Heather Muir's grand-daughter, Mrs A H Chambers, and her husband, and some of the unusual plants to be seen in the gardens are available in the plant sales area.

From the terrace there are spectacular views over the countryside to the Malvern Hills, and the edge is guarded by a splendid rose, 'Fruhlingsgold', which has abundant blooms in June. In spring the white sunken garden is a mass of flowering bulbs, and its wide beds are full of shrubs intended to provide a year-

KIFTSGATE COURT
Gloucestershire

3 MILES (5 KM) NORTH-EAST OF CHIPPING CAMPDEN

Part of the formal garden at Kiftsgate

round display of colour. Among the white roses is *R. sericea* 'Heather Muir', a single, early-flowering shrub which grows up to 12ft (3.5m) in height, while drifts of daffodils add seasonal colour to the drive. Among the shrub roses, *R. Wilmottiae* has small pinky-mauve flowers, but the glory of the rose border is *R. filipes* 'Kiftsgate', a white rose which, when last measured, was 80ft (24m) by 90ft (27.5m) and 50ft (15m) high.

Some of the other features of Kiftsgate are the perennial geraniums, a large wisteria and some large species of hydrangea. Equally attractive is a small enclosure, approached beneath a whitebeam archway, which is devoted to ferns and ornamental grasses. In the autumn Japanese maples shine out brightly from the bluebell wood.

The north border, too, has gold and silver plants flowering on a steep bank and, as you descend the hill to the lower garden down a very steep zig-zag path, there are tall Scots pines surrounding an informally paved area provided with seats.

Open from April to September on selected days. Tel: 0386 438777.

KNIGHTSHAYES COURT
Devon

BOLHAM, 2 MILES (3 KM) NORTH OF TIVERTON

*D*eep in the luxuriant Devon countryside north of Tiverton is one of this century's great gardens. Although the house at Knightshayes was designed in typically eccentric style by William Burges in 1870, and the framework of the garden established at that time by Edward Kemp, it was Sir John and Lady Heathcoat Amory who undertook the planning and planting from 1945. Now owned by the National Trust, the 50 acre (20ha) garden is, perhaps, most famous for the Paved and Pool Gardens and for the beautiful Garden in a Wood, created by Sir Eric Savill and Norman Hadden and regarded by many as their masterpiece.

The garden at Knightshayes is approached through the former stable block, which today serves as the Trust's shop, restaurant and plant nursery, and then via the north-western corner of the house towards the conservatory. Against the house is a magnificent *Magnolia grandiflora* 'Exmouth', and a quince which produces large red flowers during the spring and spherical yellow fruits. From this top terrace you can appreciate the way in which the garden relates directly to the countryside to the south, and at the end of the terrace a border includes dianthus, artemisias and veronicas, as well as an attractive mauve sage.

Beyond a short flight of steps there is a yew hedge sculpted by Sir Ian Heathcoat Amory to form a hunting scene in topiary, and raised beds of alpines lead into the Paved Garden. The theme of this striking 'garden room' is silver, with dwarf geraniums breaking up the harsh pattern of the paving. There is also a fine lead cistern

Battlemented yew hedges surround the lily pool

filled with plants. Assisted by the late Lanning Roper, Sir John and Lady Heathcoat Amory have transformed a bowling green into a serene water garden featuring a circular waterlily pool. It is surrounded by battlemented yew hedges and a single weeping pear which contrasts with the late summer leaves of an *Acer pseudoplatanus* 'Brilliantissimum' peering over the hedge.

The Garden in a Wood is a triumph of balance. The beeches, oaks and larches have been carefully thinned to let in sufficient light to enable bold-coloured and delicately shaded rhododendrons and azaleas – underplanted with crocus, narcissus, cyclamen and trilliums – to flower, depending on the season. Hostas, irises and euphorbias flourish, of course, but there are sun-lovers, such as phormiums from New Zealand, as well as climbing roses, honeysuckle and clematis. Beyond the wood is an open lawn planted with birch, a glade, and a lower border holding sages, hostas and meconopsis. Sir John's Wood has many larches and evergreens, while the extension to the South Garden includes a number of striking dogwoods, as well as Japanese cherries which give dramatic colour in spring.

Open daily from April to October. Tel: 0884 254665

A winding path shows the way to the woodland garden

SNOWSHILL MANOR
Gloucestershire

3 MILES (5 KM) SOUTH OF BROADWAY

A shaggy-browed,
ornamental water-spout

Situated on a Cotswold hillside with spectacular views over some of the most beautiful countryside in Gloucestershire, Snowshill Manor gardens were built as a series of inter-connecting 'rooms', in the manner of Hidcote (see page 38). The owner, Charles Wade, was himself an architect and a devotee of the Arts and Crafts ideals popularised by William Morris, but in 1919 he commissioned another architect of like mind, M H Baillie-Scott, to transform what he called 'a wilderness of chaos' into the series of terraces, the Armillary Court, the shrubbery and the Well Garden, as well as the kitchen gardens we see now. Wade was an obsessive collector of items of craftsmanship – bicycles, musical instruments, clocks, Chinese lacquer cabinets, and many other things – which he placed in the manor house although he actually lived until his death in 1956 in a small cottage called The Priest's House. Today, the National Trust owns Snowshill, displays Wade's eccentric collections and maintains the charming country garden to its usual high standard.

To the left of the terrace garden there is a very beautiful double border, one side of which is bright with red

Oriental and yellow Welsh poppies, while the other has potentillas along a wooden fence. On the wall a potato vine and other climbers are artfully trained, while the bold lines of espaliered fruit trees – apples, pears and figs – stand out in tempting fashion.

Charles Wade had a special love of blue, and seats and woodwork throughout the gardens at Snowshill are painted with a shade of 'Wade' blue – a powdery dark blue with a touch of turquoise. There can be no doubt that this blue harmonises well with the Cotswold stone walls, and is a particularly unassertive colour in a landscape setting, as well as providing a foil for the mauves and purples which are used to such good effect here.

A spring rising under the manor house feeds several small basins, a fountain and pools, and a lovely pink shrub rose grows over the old well-head. Behind one of the former cow byres is a tall, white guelder rose, *Vibernum opulus*, underplanted with hostas, gunnera and ferns. As you climb the steps near the shrubbery the path is overhung with weeping cherries, and there is a strong atmosphere here of the Victorian romantic garden.

Open from April to October on selected days. Tel: 0386 852410.

Stone steps lead down from the upper garden, past the Irish yews and a magnificent philadelphus

STOURTON HOUSE
Wiltshire

STOURTON, 2 MILES (3 KM) NORTH-WEST OF MERE

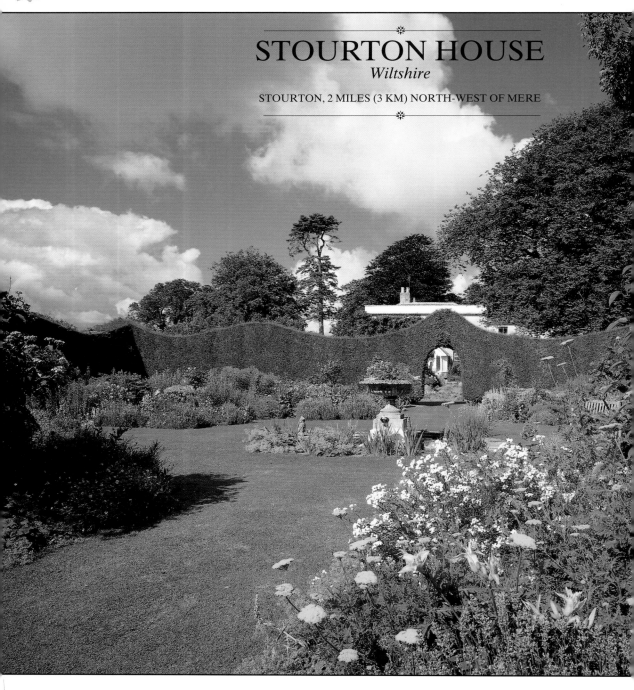

Borders colourful with golden achillea in the gardens at Stourton

*I*t says much for the charm and beauty of Stourton House gardens that they can stand comparison with the magnificent landscaped grounds of Stourhead only a matter of 300 yards away. In 5 acres (2ha) many plant treasures, accommodated in a series of small, friendly spaces, are to be seen. Stourton is also a garden with a purpose: to produce flowers and foliage for drying, with up to 70 per cent of the plants produced being dried and turned into beautiful bouquets.

There is a historical connection between the two gardens as, in late Georgian times, a parson of Stourton married one of the Miss Hoares of Stourhead and money from the banking family went into constructing Stourton House and laying out a garden. But it was not until Colonel and Mrs Bullivant came to live here 30 years ago, and flower-drying became the business of the house, that the gardens really took on their present character.

Now the main gardens lie on the east side of the house, and visitors are recommended to start their tour in the kitchen garden where the beds contain not only vegetables, but also a range of

Bog plants include the carnivorous pitcher plant, flowering rushes and groups of lovely water iris, both yellow and purple, and around the margins are rock roses, mimulus and carnations. The surrounding beds are overflowing with tree peonies, hydrangeas, standard roses, perennial honesty, and the meadow foam offers colour throughout the season.

To the south of the Pool Garden is the Lower Pond Garden, where daffodils and narcissus dominate in spring, and near by there is a pocket handkerchief tree, *Davidia involucrata*, and a splendid *Magnolia liliiflora* 'Nigra', which boasts purple flowers. Beyond the south lawn and the 19th-century greenhouse, perhaps a relic of the link with the Hoare family, is a woodland garden covered in hostas and different species of hydrangea.

This is a fascinating garden, with meandering paths through the different sections giving constant surprise and interest. Many plants have self-seeded, like the brightly coloured poached-egg plant, to give Stourton a true cottage feel as well as a formal one.

Open from April to November, on selected days.

The flame-coloured nasturtium Tropaeolum speciosum grows spectacularly in the hedge

flowers suitable for drying, including Love Lies Bleeding, *Amaranthus caudatus*, pretty poppies, Chinese lanterns, teasels and achillea. It is here that you will also see some of the 200 varieties of hydrangea – blues and whites, creams and pinks – for which Stourton is famous.

On either side of the path leading down to the Lily Pond garden are great Lawson cypresses known as the Twelve Apostles. The central pool is surrounded by beds of shrubs and herbaceous plants, while the flower fountain in the centre consists of a stone dish filled with unusual plants.

TINTINHULL HOUSE GARDENS
Somerset

TINTINHULL, 4 MILES (6.5 KM) NORTH-WEST OF YEOVIL

A catmint-bordered path leads through the decorative kitchen garden to the orchard

In many ways, the layout at Tintinhull is perfect. It so perfectly complements the 1630 house that one feels that the design must originally date from the same period, and yet it was created during the present century, largely by Mrs Phyllis Reiss who lived here for 28 years. Then again, so skilful is the arrangement of walled and hedged enclosures, the placing of important trees, and the vistas, that the garden seems much larger than its 2 acres (1ha). When to these remarkable qualities are added borders planted for all-year-round interest and designed with the texture

and shape of plants in mind, it is clear that, in the hands of Penelope Hobhouse, wife of the present tenant of the National Trust, Tintinhull is one of the most interesting gardens in the south of England.

The main axis of the garden runs from the five-bayed west front of the house through three compartments to the western boundary, while a path crosses this line at the fountain and passes through the kitchen garden to the orchard. Further strong design elements are provided by the great Cedar of Lebanon in Cedar Court, which is a broad, asymmetrical shape, and the two holm oaks which interrupt the view to the south-west and create the backdrop to the Pool Garden.

The garden can be approached either from the house or by way of the north front above Cedar Court, through an arch. The four plots are planted with regal lilies that flower in early summer and with box domes which have been in their present positions since the 1930s. On the north side are choisyas, honeysuckles, roses, agapanthus and rosemary, while on the west there are several varieties of clematis and tree peonies. To the south, begonias and a perennial honesty predominate, and on the east side are lovely groups of lavender, including ' Hidcote', a variety named after the garden that has provided so much of the inspiration for Tintinhull.

The central garden has a further series of box domes, but here hydrangeas and roses are the main features. Azaleas are planted in beds on either side of the central path in the next enclosure, which in spring and early summer is alive with colourful bulbs, including *Anemone apennina*. The Pool Garden and its pavilion were constructed by Mrs Reiss in 1947 in memory of her nephew, a pilot killed during the war. The west border is full of hot colours which contrast with the border on the other side of the canal where the themes are soft greys and silver foliage.

Open from April to September, on selected days. Tel: 0985 847777.

Tall yew hedges offset silvery grey foliage, looking back towards the house

TREBAH
Cornwall

MAWNAN SMITH, 3 MILES (5 KM) SOUTH OF FALMOUTH

*E*ven by Cornish standards, the gardens of Trebah are remarkable. Covering 25 acres (10ha), they occupy a ravine some 500yds long which runs from a fine 18th-century house at its head to a private beach on the Helford River, dropping more than 200ft (61m) in the process. Its original creator, Charles Fox, came to Trebah in 1826, and to shelter the ravine from the fierce coastal winds he planted a great screen of maritime pines, *Pinus pinaster*, behind which seeds and plants collected from all over the world could flourish.

A stream runs through a water garden in the upper part of Trebah, created since 1981 by the present owners, Major and Mrs Hibbert, who have also placed the gardens in a charitable Trust to ensure that this extraordinary conception cannot die in the future. Small pools edged with primulas and water irises, astilbes and ligularias, bamboo and ferns give colour and form to the scene, while the lower part of the ravine supports the largest *Gunnera manicata* (Brazilian rhubarb) that most people are ever likely to see.

A dense network of paths leads either down in to the valley, just a short way down to the Koi Pool and waterfall, or along the Camellia Walk to a viewpoint overlooking the beach. Below, many species of rhododendron flower in the spring and early summer. Some, including 'Trebah Gem', which was planted in 1900, have now reached 45ft (13m) in height, while two R. *'Loderi'* 'King George' have delicate pink buds which open in May as large white, fragrant blooms.

Trebah is famous for its tender trees and shrubs. A large Chilean laurel with bright green, aromatic leaves can be seen in the Chilean Combe, and the dogwood, 'Bentham's Cornel', with its yellow bracts, does well. Magnolias, including *Magnolia x soulangiana*, and the pink tulip tree, are also well represented, as are many varieties of eucalyptus, pieris and tree ferns. Three extremely tall Chusan palm trees dominate the view down the ravine, and you can also see a pocket handkerchief tree and an exotic though actually quite hardy Chinese fir. Alas, when temperatures fell to -15°C in January 1987 Trebah lost many beautiful trees, including the largest *Eucalyptus overta* in England and a *Rhododendron sinograndes*, which was thought to be more than a hundred years old.

Special care has been taken to extend the flowering season of the garden right through to Christmas with acres of blue and white hydrangeas.

Open daily from April to August. Tel: 0326 250448.

Left, the three tall Chusan palms dominate the view down the valley

Below, exotic tree ferns fill the old quarry

TRESCO ABBEY GARDENS
Tresco, Isles of Scilly

A brilliant cluster of South African lampranthus

Few gardens are reached by a more exciting journey than the Abbey Gardens on Tresco, one of the Isles of Scilly. There is a choice of either taking the *Scillonian* from Penzance, and then a launch from St Mary's, or a helicopter – also from Penzance – that goes direct to the garden gates. The gardens represent a remarkable work of construction by their founder, Augustus Smith, in 1834, and they are maintained today by his descendant, the present owner, R A Dorrien Smith.

Tresco lies in the Atlantic 30 miles (48km) off the coast of Cornwall and is warmed by the Gulf Stream. Although the temperatures in winter rarely fall below 10°C, exceptional sub-zero temperatures in January 1987 caused terrible damage to some of the sub-tropical plants. Of course, the wind is an ever-present enemy, and with great forethought, Augustus Smith provided his three great terraces, the Long Walk and the Middle and Top Terraces, with shelter-belts of Monterey cypress, tall hedges of holm oak and high, retaining walls. These also provide an effective setting for the granite house that he built near the ruins of a Benedictine priory.

The 14 acre (5.5ha) gardens are home to many exotic plants, including the South African proteus, the tender geranium from Madeira, *G. maderense,* tall date palms from the Canary Islands and the striking Chilean *Myrtus luma* which has orange-coloured bark. There are also acacias, eucalyptus and the New Zealand *Metrosideros tomentosa* which is 80ft

(24m) tall, has a great number of aerial roots and produces crimson flowers in summer.

Around St Nicholas's Priory honeysuckles, the blue-flowering *Convolvulus mauritanicus* and the pretty Mexican daisy spill out of cracks in the ancient walls and arches, and there is a magnificent rock garden excavated into a 40ft (12m) cliff below. The Middle Terrace has an area known as Mexico, and is covered with the turquoise flowers of *Puya alpestris* from Chile. Further along, a stone summerhouse is overgrown with Burmese honeysuckle.

Tresco Abbey gardens offer many unusual delights, but no visitor should miss the so-called Valhalla. Open on one side, the building houses some of the figureheads of ships that have foundered on the treacherous rocks of the Isles of Scilly during the last three centuries.

Open daily, all year. Tel: 0720 22849.

Above, the exotic flower of a King protea

Left, a different sort of garden ornament – a ship's figurehead from 'Valhalla'

TREWITHEN
Cornwall

7 MILES (11 KM) WEST OF ST AUSTELL

The long sweep of lawn flanked by trees, including a 55ft magnolia, makes an impressive setting for early 18th-century Trewithen House

The word 'Trewithen' is Cornish for 'House in the Spinney', and the mature trees of the 18th-century park have undoubtedly offered protection from the coastal winds, enabling many tender plants to flourish here. George Johnstone inherited the property in 1904 and

campbellii mollicomata, more than 55ft (17m) high and covered with large pink blooms in early March. Close to it is the tulip tree, whose blooms are a slightly deeper shade of pink, while other favourites, *M. liliiflora*, with purplish, pink flowers, and *M. x soulangiana*, are also present.

devoted the rest of his life to creating and maintaining the 28 acre (11ha) garden, which occupies a level site 250 feet (76m) above sea level. A great hybridist, he played an important part in the development of the popular *Camellia x williamsii* 'Donation', but his first love was magnolias, and the Royal Horticultural Society published his magisterial work, *Asiatic Magnolias in Cultivation*, in 1955. Many of Johnstone's plants are still to be seen today at Trewithen, and this wonderful garden is now owned by his grandson, Michael Galsworthy.

It is ironical that The Glade, perhaps the most admired part of Trewithen, came about as a result of a government order during World War I to fell 300 trees. The lawn stretches for over 200yds to the south of the house, but the first part of this magnificent amphitheatre is dominated by one of the garden's great trees, *Magnolia*

Further south is a group of hybrid rhododendrons, including 'Alison Johnstone' (named after George Johnstone's wife); the Chilean fire bush, which turns completely scarlet in May; a coral-bark maple; and a fine southern beech – a conical tree whose leaves change to orange and red in autumn.

Camellias play an important part in the woodland garden to the west of The Glade lawn. 'Trewithen Pink' can be seen, as can 'Elizabeth Johnstone', named after Mr Johnstone's daughter, and a camellia with a single pink bloom named after the present owner's late wife, 'Charlotte Galsworthy'. Shrubs, including viburnums, azaleas, potentillas, euonymus and berberis, edge the lawn in front of the house. The walled garden, which is covered with tender plants, surrounds a pool, while a wisteria-draped pergola adds colour to this formal area. Recently planted beds of birch and sorbus, mahonia, dogwoods and roses, heathers and conifers help to make Trewithen not only an outstanding plant collection, but a place of ever-changing variety and colour.

Open from March to September, on selected days. Tel: 0726 882418 or 882763.

Among the plants that George Johnstone bred is a hybrid rhododendron 'Alison Johnstone' named after his wife

VINE HOUSE
Avon

HENBURY, 4 MILES (6.5 KM) NORTH-WEST OF BRISTOL

The orchard may be glimpsed through the greenery, with the church tower beyond

Close to the centre of Bristol, Vine House has the good fortune to be on the edge of the Blaise Castle estate – which was landscaped by Humphry Repton – alongside the Hazel Brook, a tributary of the River Trym. Even allowing for the well-wooded acres of the 18th-century park, the immediate urban surroundings of The Vine are somewhat unprepossessing, but once behind the creeper-clad stone house it is easy to see what appealed to Professor T F Hewer and his wife, Anne, when they first began to design the layout in 1946.

The 2 acre (0.8ha) garden is divided roughly into two parts: the upper lawn is given a wonderful sense of enclosure and shape by the two magnolias – one against the house and the other near the stables – by the great mulberry, and by tall conifers standing at the back of the herbaceous border. Further down a stream, bright with colourful bog plants such as *Lysichiton americanus* and irises, flows over rocks, past a small arbour and under a stone bridge to the slow-moving brook. In the lower part of the garden the owners have created a peaceful green glade with spring bulbs, cyclamen, and an abundance of hostas, cistus and gunnera.

In two respects Vine House is an important as well as a beautiful garden. When they started work, Professor and Mrs Hewer reduced the site to bare earth and planned the position and eventual size of the trees with the help of sticks topped by pieces of white paper. As the head of the Department of Pathology, Professor Hewer regularly travelled abroad to conferences and brought back with him specimen trees which have now matured. Carefully labelled and dated, the trees at Vine House constitute a remarkable arboretum, including as they do a 30ft (9m)

Metasequoia glyptostroboides and a splendid weeping pine from Yugoslavia, introduced in 1951 and now underplanted with cyclamen. Together with Chinese specimens, a Japanese cherry, and a noble *Acer capillipes* grown from seed obtained from the Westonbirt Arboretum in 1957, this is an important collection of trees in its own right.

Vine House is a memorable garden at any stage of the year, but particularly so in the spring and early summer. When the bulbs are at their best, the garden boasts an unusually tall snowdrop with bell-shaped, white flowers on a leafless stem. Then, as the days lengthen, a pale smoke bush and hybrid tree peonies take over, filling this peaceful woodland garden with subtle colour.

Open from April to May, on selected days. Tel: 0272 503573.

Left, a comfortably overgrown path and a profusion of flowers (below) characterise this charming garden

BENINGTON LORDSHIP
Hertfordshire

BENINGTON, 4 MILES (6.5 KM) EAST OF STEVENAGE

A brilliant show of colour in the deep herbaceous borders

Benington Lordship is one of those rare gardens which has almost all the advantages. Situated near Stevenage, it occupies a site that has been inhabited since the Norman Conquest, and can boast a keep which dates from the 11th century, a moat which is covered with snowdrops in early spring, fine views over the surrounding countryside, a colourful rockery and large herbaceous borders.

In 1905, when the present owner's grandfather, Arthur Bott, bought the property, there was no garden, and the area now occupied by the park and garden was a nine-hole golf course. As well as enlarging the house, Mr Bott created a garden with a characteristic Edwardian flavour which is still maintained by Mr and Mrs C H A Bott and their head gardener, Ian Billot. Benington Lordship stands 400 feet (122m) above sea level on heavy clay, so that the beds have to be heavily mulched with compost and manure. Much of the grass is not cut until the full summer, and in consequence the gardens are famous for their spring colour, with drifts of snowdrops, scillas, cowslips and garlic.

In front of the house, the Rose Garden has been replanted with the fragrant, bluish-white rose 'Margaret Merril' and with 'Radox

This curious figure of Shylock emerges from a sea of white 'Iceberg' roses

Bouquet'. Along the verandah, which recalls Arthur Bott's time in India, is a collection of yellow shrub roses, including 'Agnes', the fragrant *Rosa primula*, the incense rose, and 'Fruhlingsdrift'. From the west end of the house there are splendid views over the old entrance drive, and a large urn, found in the moat, has been surrounded by a camomile lawn and by *Rosa moyesii* 'Geranium'. Beyond the urn, a path leads into the moat, past a number of crab apple trees and cowslip and heather banks.

The rockery was planned during World War I around a spring in the top pool, and now, once the early bulbs are over, it displays attractive groups of primulas, herbs and alliums.

Set surprisingly far away from the house, two wonderfully deep borders run east to west below the kitchen garden and plant centre. Interrupted by fine, brick gate-piers, the borders are bright in summer with rock roses, sedums, salvias and potentillas. At Benington Lordship, the kitchen garden still grows vegetables, while, backing on to the herbaceous border are beds full of the most wonderful autumn colour, one overflowing with Michaelmas daisies – so popular a plant during Edwardian times.

Open from April to September, on selected afternoons. Tel: 043 885 668.

BETH CHATTO GARDENS
Essex

6 MILES (9.5 KM) EAST OF ELMSTEAD MARKET, COLCHESTER

A perfect harmony of landscape and planting has been achieved by the water

No one who has seen Beth Chatto's display gardens at the Chelsea Flower Show can doubt that she is one of the most influential gardeners of our time, and a visit to her own gardens at Elmstead Market more than confirms this view. In her book *The Dry Garden*, Mrs Chatto emphasises that she selects each plant or tree 'for its shape and character, not for the colour of its flowers', and this respect for the habit of plants is the dominant impression you gain on entering the gardens.

Before 1960 there was neither house nor garden on the site, and with just a few trees in place, Mrs Chatto gradually converted the problem areas into gardens of different characters: the dry gravel parts are filled with drought-resistant plants bright with warm colours; a woodland garden lies in the shade of tall trees; and water gardens have been made where it was boggy before. These distinct types of garden now show an astonishing range of plants.

where a winding path meanders between lush shade-loving plants such as ferns, hostas, spotted pulmonarias and the elegant Solomon's seal, underplanted by the delicate purple-leaved violet.

Below, in a series of four pools surrounded by bog gardens, are some tall plants – angelicas, rodgersias, irises, the umbrella plant and bright yellow trollius. Bog arums and the

Initially, Mr and Mrs Chatto tackled the gravel areas which surround the house, and they constructed the Mediterranean Garden. The raised beds show bold contrasts of form and colour provided by plants like silver-leaved santolinas, artemisias, and variegated and purple-leaved sages. A Mount Etna broom with a fountain of tiny yellow, deliciously scented pea flowers dominates shrub planting of cistus, buddleia and many other species.

Leaving the warm Mediterranean Garden, there is a transformation in the cool grass beneath the tall oaks,

giant gunneras contrast with candelabra primulas, water forget-me-not, and *Pontederia cordata*, while, further away, but still enjoying the damp conditions, astilbes are underplanted with hostas. Where the pools narrow to a canal, bushes of *Viburnum plicatum* 'Mariesii' are loaded with white flowers in spring, while irises, ferns and New Zealand flax flourish in company with marsh marigolds, senecios and pink polygonum.

Open from March to October, Monday to Saturday, and from November to February, Monday to Friday. Tel: 0206 222007.

Floral beds with hemerocalis, astilbes, delphiniums and filipendula curve away into the distance

BROUGHTON CASTLE
Oxfordshire

2 MILES (3 KM) SOUTH-WEST OF BANBURY

The borders at Broughton preserve the colour scheme originally devised by Gertrude Jekyll

Standing just to the south of Banbury in the lush Oxfordshire countryside, Broughton Castle is a castellated manor house which was greatly enlarged in the middle of the 16th century. The house itself is built of a beautiful, honey-coloured Hornton ironstone, and with its intimate 3 acre (1ha) garden is romantically surrounded by a large moat. In 1900 there were no less than 14 gardeners at Broughton, but Lord and Lady Saye and Sele and their young gardener, Randal Anderson, have simplified the structure while preserving the grandeur of the setting. In this, the owners were greatly assisted by the late Lanning Roper who, in 1969, suggested opening up the views across the park, and the gardens now consist of two magnificent borders and an enclosed, formal parterre.

Backed by a 14th-century stone wall, the Battlement Border has a colour scheme of blue and yellow, white and grey. Here, the main shrub roses are 'Marigold', a vigorous climber with semi-double bronze-yellow blooms, 'Golden Wings', the fragrant, apricot-coloured 'Buff Beauty', and a new rose, 'Windrush'. The west-facing border also holds *Campanula lactiflora*, willow herb, the creamy-white flowers of *Philadelphus* 'Manteau d'Hermine' and hypericum. The other long border concentrates its colours on pink and red through to white, with *Rosa* 'Fantin-Latour' set against potentillas, eupatoriums and philadelphus.

The enclosed formal layout is the square Ladies' Garden, and here borders on the west side flank walls which are all that remain of the 16th-century kitchens, the mullioned windows bearing testimony to the

original purpose of the building. Laid out originally about a century ago, there are four fleur-de-lis beds surrounded by miniature box hedges. These are furnished with floribunda roses, including 'Gruss en Aachen', and two circular beds contain lavender. Against the castle wall is a fine display of the double, pale-pink flowers of *Rosa* 'Felicia', and there are mixed borders on both sides of this lovely enclosure. Everywhere at Broughton is a wonderful profusion of old-fashioned roses and sweeping flows of colour. The harmony that has been achieved between the serenity of the castle itself and the beauty of its garden setting adds greatly to the pleasure of a visit to this most English of castles.

Open from May to September on selected afternoons, and other times by appointment. Tel: 0295 262624/812027.

The Ladies' Garden, glimpsed through an archway

CHENIES MANOR HOUSE
Buckinghamshire

4 MILES (6.5 KM) EAST OF AMERSHAM

The hot reds and pinks of chrysanthemums and nicotiana warm this bed and are shown off richly against the dark green foliage

Standing deep in the luxuriant Chiltern countryside some 200ft (61m) above the River Chess is the small village of Chenies. There must have been a house here from the earliest times, but the present brick-built manor house dates in the most part from 1460. Over a century later the owner was Lucy, 3rd Countess of Bedford, who enjoyed a considerable reputation as a gardener, and the layout of the gardens that she established continued to be followed, although the house ceased to be the family's principal seat, and neglect set in during the 18th century. Today, the present owners, Lt Col Alastair MacLeod Matthews and his wife, Elizabeth, have restored these beautiful gardens as the background to a family home.

At the rear of the house we find one of the most enchanting arrangements of little gardens, enclosed by neatly cut yew hedges. Facing the Tudor ruin of what was once children's nurseries is a lawn bounded on one side by an attractive border of shrub roses, including 'Felicia', 'Cornelia' and 'Buff Beauty'. Beyond this is a most charming 'garden room' with a lawn surrounded by a pink and white border. Spidery, delicate cleomes contrast with broad-petalled cosmos in different shades of pink, interplanted with white nicotianas, while, lower down, there is a gentle edging of *Alchemilla mollis*.

Through an archway you enter a sunken garden, which is built on the same plan as the Privy Garden at Hampton Court. In spring, hundreds of colourful tulips and other bulbs catch the eye, while later on in the season warm shades of annuals and perennials take over. Begonias, dahlias, heliotrope and marguerites are neatly held together by box hedges, and, in the middle, a small pond completes the picture.

Leaving the sunken garden, you enter the Physic Garden which boasts an extensive collection of herbs surrounding an octagonal wellhouse built in 1821. Although the collection has been created recently by Elizabeth MacLeod Matthews, it echoes the common medieval practice of growing herbs for medicinal purposes, for scent and dye, and for flavouring otherwise tasteless food. Lugwort, Jacob's ladder and rose madder rub shoulders with

fennel, dill and chives, while there are also rarities such as Madagascar periwinkle and datura to be found.

On the opposite side of the Physic Garden, beyond an avenue of clipped yew and Lawson cypresses leading to a sundial, you reach the White Garden. Completely enclosed and with a pleached lime walk on the south side, it is planted with white, grey and green shrubs, perennials and annuals, centred on a lead statue of Cupid. Dogtooth violets, muscari, viburnums, hydrangeas, convolvulus, geraniums and white agapanthus appear in their respective seasons.

The east lawn is surrounded by roses and shaded by a weeping ash, while the border closest to the house in the South Garden is bright with hemerocallis 'Stella d'Oro', lychnis and penstemon 'Garnet', and there is also a collection of spectacular lilies. Near the entrance to the orchard and kitchen garden is a recreated turf maze, or labyrinth, built originally as an aid to prayer. A gravel walk leads to a potager, or decorative vegetable garden, constructed in the French manner.

Open from April to October, on selected afternoons. Tel: 049476 2888.

Looking into the delightful sunken garden, with its ornamental box hedges

Delphiniums of deepest blue

DENMANS
West Sussex

FONTWELL, 4½ MILES (7 KM) EAST OF CHICHESTER

Nestling below the South Downs is the beautiful 3½ acre (1.5ha) garden of Denmans. Like all really distinguished gardens, it is continually changing and repays regular visits by both plant lovers and those interested in garden design, because, since 1985, it has been managed by the landscape designer and author, John Brookes. Mrs Joyce Robinson, the present owner, and her husband, bought the estate in 1946, and with the exception of a great cedar of Lebanon, planted in the early 19th century, and some old pears, all the trees that give the garden its form today have been introduced by Mrs Robinson.

At the end of the gravel path leading from the car park, the planting is striking and individual. A great clump of euphorbias grows outside

Planting of blue and silver gives way to white and gold

the tea shop, while in a nearby bed viburnums, weigela and laurel flourish, fringed by achilleas, purple sage and lady's mantle. Four foliage beds have also been planted, rather like a colour-coding for the main garden. In the first bed the theme is silver and white, so *Lamium* 'Molten Silver', hebes, *Stachys lanata* and verbascums predominate. The red bed shows *Berberis thunbergii,* a dark-leaved bergenia and an elder, while the two remaining beds are devoted to gold plants and to a collection of grasses.

The conservatory houses tender plants, with clematis 'Vyvyan Pennell' showing mauve flowers in spring, contrasting with two beautiful abutilons, one peach-coloured and the other red. Over the entrance to the nearby walled garden, *Clematis montana* 'Rubrum' cascades, and the sinuous gravel path and the dense planting soon transports you into another world, one dominated by a tall *Eucalyptus gunnii* underplanted with honeysuckle, philadelphus, purple lilac and a robust yellow peony.

The main garden slopes south, with a large lawn broken up by a dry gravel 'stream' that runs down to a pond. At the top is a splendid group of trees which includes a cherry and a whitebeam. Stone bridges cross the 'stream', and bamboo and willow grow alongside viburnums, phormiums and the Mexican orange blossom. Instead of pebbles, the pond is filled with water, and waterlilies punctuate its surface. Among the trees are a *Cupressus arizonica*, a great dawn redwood, a ginkgo and a tulip tree, as well as two red oaks shading a small orchard. Here, sitting on a seat in a sunny corner, is an ideal place to admire the beauty and the design of this most charming and diverse of gardens.

Open daily, from March to December. Tel: 0243 542808.

A small statue sits patiently beside the lily pond

GREAT COMP
Kent

BOROUGH GREEN, 7 MILES (11 KM) EAST OF SEVENOAKS

S ited in the beautiful wooded countryside of the Weald of Kent, Great Comp gardens surround a 17th-century house. Mr and Mrs Roderick Cameron originally bought an area of 4¹/₂ acres (2ha), but land was added in 1962 and 1975 so that today the gardens cover 7¹/₂ acres (3ha). Considerable devastation was caused by the great storms of 1987 and 1990, but Great Comp remains a successful combination of a plantsman's garden, with over 3000 named plants (including no fewer than 30 varieties of magnolia), and one of changing vistas employing curving walks through colourful woodland and focal points such as a group of ruins, a temple and several urns.

Entering on the north side of the garden you come on to a spacious lawn sloping up to a top terrace. Viburnums predominate in the shrub and herbaceous border, and the old yew, *Taxus baccata*, is thought to be more than 150 years old. Two young ginkgoes stand on either side of the steps with a *Photinia x fraseri* close by. The borders here are planted in a cottage-garden style, and although you would expect to find plants like phloxes and violas in such a setting,

The back of the house overlooks an expanse of well kept lawn, deeply cut with beds and borders

angel's fishing rods, crocosmias and yuccas are, perhaps, more of a surprise. Several berberis make an attractive impact, as does golden sage, variegated thyme and rue. On the top path the planting of the borders is rich, with colourful azaleas, hydrangeas, Japanese witch hazel and many varieties of magnolia. In the woodland in this eastern part of the garden are a tall silver birch, *Pinus sylvestris* 'Aurea' and a red oak, while beyond a fine American dogwood is a splendid young dawn redwood.

One of the pleasures of Great Comp is the sudden appearance of long views in the depths of beautiful woodland. From the Lion Summerhouse, a tastefully converted privy, there is a splendid view of the garden's 'Place de l'Etoile', embellished with a Doulton urn. In the same area, the 'ruins' were created 15 years ago, and conifers, heathers and rock plants enhance their picturesque effect. At the garden's southern boundary a long, straight path joins the Vine urn with the Temple, and from this vantage point you can see both winter and summer heathers. The shrub planting includes the American smoke bush, and *Pinus coulteri* with its abnormally long needles. Near the Temple, erected in 1973, is a wonderful weeping pear, as well as a Nootka cypress.

Returning to the house a *Magnolia x veitchii* can be seen underplanted with hostas, ferns, irises, lysimachia and polygonum, and in the herbaceous borders in the Square, plume poppies, pink, yellow and white achillea, sedums, euonymus, yuccas and begonias add their seasonal colour.

Open daily, from April to October. Tel: 0732 882669.

Above, a pathway of surprises in the ornamental woodland

Below, a hydrangea has been underplanted and invaded by brilliant nasturtiums

GREAT DIXTER
East Sussex

NORTHIAM, 7 MILES (11 KM) NORTH-WEST OF RYE

The name of Great Dixter will be familiar to all who read Christopher Lloyd's regular contributions on gardening in *Country Life*, but the lively inventiveness of his horticultural style none the less comes as a surprise however often you visit the garden. The medieval manor was bought by Nathaniel Lloyd in 1910, and Sir Edwin Lutyens was commissioned to design the gardens, and the steps and terraces that still provide the framework of the layout are distinctly his. The sunken garden, the topiary and the yew and box hedging were the responsibility of the owner, while his wife, Daisy, created the wild moat garden and continued to help develop the garden in conjunction with her son, Christopher, after her husband's death.

The gardens at Dixter totally surround the 15th-century manor house, and the lane from Northiam brings you to the north side, a flagstone path leading straight through a lovely meadow area to the medieval porch. In summer yellow and orange lilies grow in pots to brighten the timber-framed façade, while ferns flourish beneath the windows, and the lawn supports a Chilean bamboo and an old common pear. Near by, on this north side, is the colourful sunken garden with an octagonal pool

Left, the timber-framed manor house provides an attractive focus for this country garden

Above, a flash of kniphofia lends colour to the moat

surrounded by drystone walls, the enclosure framed by barn walls and a yew hedge. Ferns and Kenilworth ivy grow out of crevices in the paving, and geraniums and lavender support the rich border-planting of campanulas, astrantias, *Eryngium giganteum*, variegated euonymus, day lilies and lychnis.

In the walled garden, spare a glance for the *Clematis x jouiniana* 'Praecox', and for the blue thistles, euphorbias and mallows, before leaving via a flight of steps characteristic of Lutyens' style. Continue past a bed of hydrangeas, rodgersias and geraniums to the topiary lawn, inhabited by great birds and abstract shapes in clipped yew. The old moat is seeded with grasses and is bright in spring with moon daisies, knapweed and clover, while a splendid magnolia makes a dramatic seasonal show.

The Long Border is strong in colour contrasts, with golden elder and Mount Etna broom set against white hydrangeas, variegated golden hostas and mahonia. Sea hollies make a regular appearance, while the blue of *Campanula lactiflora*, euonymus 'Silver Queen' and pink diascias contribute to a rich display. The golden shower of *Ulmus* 'Dicksonii' attracts the eye in the middle of the border with silver-grey willows underplanted with blue veronica and purple everlasting peas.

Open from April to October, afternoons except Monday, and on other selected days. Tel: 0797 43160.

Right, the sturdy yew hedges which form the enclosures in this lovely garden were laid out by Nathaniel Lloyd to give protection to more tender plants

Below, a path of rough-cut flagstones leads through the topiary

HASCOMBE COURT
Surrey

2½ MILES (4 KM) SOUTH-EAST OF GODALMING

Broad herbaceous borders lead up to the splendidly overgrown summerhouse

Situated to the south of Godalming, Hascombe Court nestles deep in the lush Surrey countryside. The extensive gardens were originally designed by Gertrude Jekyll, and remodelled in 1928 and 1929 to enable the front entrance to the house to be properly visible. During the past 12 years, the present owners, Mr and Mrs O Poulsen, have carefully restored the layout after a period of decline.

Perhaps the most interesting contrasts at Hascombe Court are provided by the changes of level from sweeping lawns and herbaceous borders to sloping hollows and woodland walks, and also by the informality of much of the garden set against the yew hedges, terraces and seats which provide the architectural bones of the layout. Below the upper terrace on the south front, a second terrace linked by flights of stone steps at each end has as its focal point a recessed, semi-circular lily pool and fountain. Enclosed on three sides by walls, the terrace has generous flower borders and topiary, while steps lead down past a paved lavender walk to a delightful Japanese rock garden. The upper terrace extends between yew and lavender beds to a formal garden centred on a fine lead fountain group designed by Lady Hilton Young, with beds filled with tulips in the spring, followed later in the season by delphiniums, lupins and penstemons. Beyond the West Terrace a spacious lawn extends to the woodland boundary, where a circular lily pool enclosed by yew hedges terminates the view. An idyllic spring walk runs between borders of azaleas, lilies and Japanese maples to a spectacular Bamboo Stairway forming a tunnel.

At the edges of the winding paths are hybrid rhododendrons, including 'Pink Pearl' and 'Britannia', the last producing striking crimson flowers. On the lower slopes, *Rhododendron arboreum, R. thomsonii* and the early-flowering *R. praecox* flourish, and in the spring the ground beneath is carpeted with narcissi and many different kinds of flowering bulbs.

From the lower part of the garden, steps lead up to Brenda's Walk, which skirts the valley and is planted with laburnums and berberis, with orange and yellow lilies and with delphiniums. A glade leads through a wild garden with flowering crabs and cherries to a spectacular, double herbaceous border terminated at the far end by an open-fronted summerhouse.

It is one of the characteristics of Hascombe Court that the gardens not only provide a delightful setting for the house, but relate successfully to the wonderful Surrey countryside that surrounds the property.

Open from April to July, on selected days.

Terraces spread down from the house to the Japanese Rock Garden

HATFIELD HOUSE
Hertfordshire

HATFIELD

The spacious Privy Garden, surrounded by a walkway of pleached limes

Both setting and history combine to make the gardens of Hatfield House one of the most outstanding in the country. The Jacobean house was built between 1607 and 1611 by Robert Cecil, chief minister to King James 1, and this mellow brick building, together with the remaining great hall wing of the Old Palace of Hatfield, where Princess Elizabeth was confined during her sister Mary's reign, provide the backdrop for gardens that were planned by John Tradescant the Elder. Today, the gardens are fortunate in that the present Marchioness of Salisbury has set herself the task of remaking the layout as it might have been during Stuart times.

From the north court of the great house you pass directly into the West Gardens and to a border planted with yew and *Phillyrea latifolia*. Approaching the deep-red façade of

the old Palace, you look down on to the knot garden in the manner in which it might have been seen in the 17th century. The seven knots of the garden were made by Lady Salisbury in the 1980s, following an Italian design, with the outer hedges of clipped hawthorn incorporating seats over which honeysuckle has been trained. The knot hedges themselves are of box with small cones at the corners, and are filled with spring bulbs that are succeeded by flowering plants and shrubs later in the season. Crown imperials, tulips, anenomes and violets bloom here in the spring, beside hellebores and the blossom of both almond and cherry trees, while in summer shrub roses contrast in shape and colour with delphiniums and pinks.

Yew hedges border the Privy Garden, and there is a pleached lime walk on all four sides. In springtime

The beautiful knot garden incorporates a maze

the beds are filled with tulips, wallflowers and polyanthus in contrast to euphorbias and hellebores. Later, peonies and mauve and red penstemons come into flower, and old shrub roses give height to the planting. Further on you descend into the scented garden, with walks between beds of camomile, lavender and thyme, and a herb garden with a central sundial. A beautiful wisteria hangs over a seat, and there are also several varieties of philadelphus, winter sweet and a fine *Mahonia japonica* to be seen.

A gate leads you into a wilderness, with winding paths through woodland that includes a Spanish chestnut (possibly dating from the 17th century), golden elms, silver birch and amelanchier. In spring this wonderful area shines with rhododendrons, camellias and magnolias underplanted with crocuses and lily of the valley. For the intrepid visitor, there are still the East Gardens to see, with a spectacular parterre, a maze, a pool garden and an orchard. Hatfield House gardens combine a magnificent historical layout with modern plantsmanship of the very highest standard.

Open daily, from late March to October. Tel: 0707 262823.

An inviting gate leads from the scented garden to the 13 acres (5ha) of wilderness

JENKYN PLACE
Hampshire

BENTLEY, 3 MILES (5 KM) WEST OF FARNHAM

The strong arches of the Dutch garden make a stunning background

Although it stands close to the main road from Farnham to Alton, in the valley of the River Wey, Jenkyn Place is a remarkably secluded garden. Even the approach, through a shaded courtyard, gives no hint of the splendour of the layout nor of the diversity of the 7 acres (3ha) of gardens that have been created by Gerald and Patricia Coke.

Once round the corner of the house you enter a small but bright Dutch garden with, in the centre, a fountain of a boy and a fish, surrounded by daphnes and four classical lead containers planted with pelargoniums and datura. Over the entrance arch climb hibiscus, tree peonies and passion flowers, and on the west-facing wall there is *Clematis* 'Niobe', with its dark-red blooms, and a myrtle 'Silver sheen' underplanted with rock roses and campanulas. Beyond is a charming terrace which offers splendid views over the end of the herbaceous borders across open countryside. It is planted with alpines in containers, a rosemary bush, and a

A splash of red plush

yellow climbing rose rambles over the wall of the dairy.

The former traditional rose garden is currently in a state of transition. It has recently been replanted in shades of purple and silver, featuring peonies and berberis among other plants. A central fountain pond is bright with waterlilies, and a Japanese medlar produces fragrant white flowers in summer. The Bowling Green is enclosed with yew hedges, while the Sundial Garden has pots of pelargoniums, a raised bed of agapanthus, South African lilies and the New Zealand burr. Like all the other individual areas of Jenkyn Place, the ornaments for the herbaceous borders have been carefully chosen to enhance the view and to act as a foil to the penstemons, centaureas, day lilies, delphiniums, phloxes and peonies that give so much summer colour.

The grassy Long Walk is backed by a rock border filled with small plants and bulbs, and from this three small gardens open. The Italian Garden contains Irish yews and a blue-and-green colour scheme, with irises and winter sweet. Then comes an area devoted to old-fashioned roses and the Yew Garden, with dwarf pines and needle grasses as well as silver and golden yews. A peony border leads to the Upper Leaf Garden, with graceful philadelphus as well as herbaceous plants – euphorbias, hellebores and pulmonarias. A berberis and an acers dominate the Lower Leaf Garden. The Armillary Sphere Garden is divided by brick paths into four squares, each with a single specimen tree – a white mulberry, a medlar, a persimmon and a cherry.

Open from April to mid-September, Thursday to Sunday. Tel: 0420 23118.

Full and varied use is made of container planting

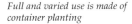

LEONARDSLEE GARDENS
West Sussex

LOWER BEEDING, 5 MILES (8 KM) SOUTH-EAST OF HORSHAM

Set in a deep woodland valley in the magnificent countryside of West Sussex, Leonardslee is one of the most spectacular gardens in England. It was created by Sir Edmund Loder at the end of the last century when rhododendrons were flooding into Britain, and not only did Sir Edmund enhance the natural beauty of Leonardslee with their dramatic colour, but hybridised the Loderi group, giving us such wonderful varieties as 'King George', 'Pink Diamond' and 'Sir Joseph Hooker'. At 70 acres (28.5ha), this is already a large garden, but Mr Robin Loder, who runs Leonardslee today, has plans to extend it into the 200 acres (81ha) of surrounding parkland.

Below the restaurant there is an umbrella-shaped cherry tree which, remarkably, has yet to be fully identified. Further down the lawn is a splendid dogwood, as well as a *Magnolia wilsonii*, a statuesque Japanese maple and a young pocket handkerchief tree, while, at the bottom, a superb group of *Rhododendron yakushimanum* creates a riot of seasonal colour. The entry to the woodland walk is marked by an evergreen azalea. This is

Rhododendrons and azaleas fill the lovely Dell

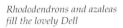

balanced by an *Acer palmatum* 'Senkaki', which has orange-yellow leaves in spring. The Loderi rhododendrons are at their best in May, but other varieties which are equally appealing are 'Carita Charm' and *R. williamsianum*. The California redwood and the Wellingtonia tower over the path, which is bright in spring both from *Camellia japonica* 'Donckelaeri' and 'Duchess of Normandy' and from beautiful magnolias.

Following the woodland path north beyond the memorial to Sir Edmund Loder you come to a superb view over the valley with gunnera on the right, and rhododendrons leading your eye down to the lakes that look so natural, but which were in fact originally hammer ponds serving the Sussex iron industry.

The path plunges steeply to a stream edged with groups of king-cups and bog arums. The rock garden, too, was constructed in about 1900 of Pulhamite, an artificial stone, to house alpines, although now it contains labour-saving azaleas, conifers and small shrubs. Mossy Ghyll contains deciduous azaleas, which have to be pruned to the ground every 15 years, and a magnificent Hungarian oak. Beyond is Hurricane Glade, so named for the losses it sustained in 1987. While the destruction of so many great trees must be regretted, it has provided a planting opportunity, which, if seized with determination, will carry these magnificent gardens into the next century.

Open on selected days from mid-April to October. Tel: 0403 891212.

Huge rhododendrons form a colourful bank beside the lake

THE MANOR HOUSE, BLEDLOW

Buckinghamshire

2½ MILES (4 KM) SOUTH-WEST OF PRINCES RISBOROUGH

The stately Manor House, with borders of roses and lavender

Nestling deep in the Buckinghamshire countryside below the Chiltern escarpment is the Manor House. A serene, brick house of the early 18th century, it stands in gardens of exceptional beauty created by the owners, Lord and Lady Carrington, with the help of the landscape architect, Robert Adams, in a style which is essentially English.

This is a garden of tremendous variety and elegance with a mixture of formal and informal enclosures. Along the width of the house, herbaceous borders planted with roses and lavender stretch out as if to emphasise the formal structure of the building, and, beyond the immaculate lawns, a line of rectangular lily ponds shows the reds, pinks and whites of many varieties of waterlily. Tall yew and beech hedges give a marvellous sense of enclosure for the yellow and white roses which contrast sharply with the blues and purples of lavender and heliotropium, while a sundial edged with box provides a central focus.

But the formal borders, filled not only with herbaceous flowers and shrubs but also with fragrant old roses, must be set against some equally enchanting informal areas. Here, you can sit and admire *Nicotiana sylvestris* towering over the bright colours of antirrhinums and fuchsias, and the stunning combination of tufts of silver santolina interplanted with purple heliotropium. Inside a walled kitchen garden, bright blue salvias, penstemons and peonies mingle with statuesque runner beans and other vegetables, and York stone paths lead to an enchanting, rose-covered gazebo.

A sculpture garden has recently been designed on a sloping site with wide open views: underneath mature trees, large modern figures playfully roll on the lawns, their white bodies contrasting with the spiky buddleia behind.

Although the gardens of the Manor House are only open on a very few days in the year, the tranquil Lyde Garden is worth going to at any time. Paths, bridges and walkways lead through this stunning water garden where there are many unusual species of plants.

Open by written appointment from May to September, and on selected afternoons. Lyde Garden is open every day.

Left, a tumbling stone figure from the sculpture garden

Below, a bench is discreetly placed to enjoy the borders

THE MANOR HOUSE
Hampshire

UPTON GREY, 6 MILES (9.5 KM) SOUTH-EAST OF BASINGSTOKE

*A*few miles to the east of Basingstoke is one of the finest garden restorations of recent years. When Mr and Mrs J Wallinger came to the Manor House, Upton Grey, in 1984, the gardens were almost derelict, but as a result of careful research and meticulous and determined work, the layout and planting conceived by Gertrude Jekyll between 1908 and 1910 is now again beginning to provide a worthy setting for the house designed by that eminent country-house architect of the Edwardian period, Ernest Newton.

Although the yew hedging still has some way to go before it can again form the bones of the garden, Mrs Wallinger obtained all 15 Jekyll plans

paths wind their way between lilac and roses, such as 'Blush Rambler', 'Jersey Beauty', 'Kitchener of Khartoum' and 'Mme d'Arbelay', while hollies, laburnum, quince and medlar, weeping ash and walnuts give shape to the layout. In the beds leading to the pond, kniphofias, hemerocallis, irises and day lilies attract the eye, naturalised daffodils give a strong start to the season, and yew, bamboo and cotinus provide the background.

On the other side of the house a pergola stands between two formal borders planted with sedums, irises, anenomes, *Asphodelus lutea* and *Penstemon* 'Glaber', and steps lead down on to a grassy parterre. The

A pink rose cascades over the pergola, above steps leading to the parterre

dated 1908/9, followed her species and cultivars when she mentioned them in the planting plan for Upton Grey, and chose early varieties or those that Jekyll is known to have liked when she only mentioned the name of the species.

Perhaps even more exciting is the re-creation of the only Jekyll wild garden known to have survived, to the south-west of the house. Here, grass steps are being put back as an entrance to the garden, and sinuous

retaining walls are bright with rock roses, campanulas, aubretia and cerastrium, while the footing beds hold choisyas, eryngiums, rosemary and nepeta. In the parterre beds, lilies and cannas are surrounded by peonies, roses and stachys, while two further deep beds have a typically cool colour scheme, provided by *Santolina incana*, lady's mantle, lavender and rosemary.

Above the rose garden, lupins, rudbeckia, delphiniums and holly-

Lilies feature strongly in the design of this garden

hocks stand behind pale spiderwort, dwarf tritona and *Nepeta mussini*, and the herbaceous borders on the other side of the garden contain coreopsis, spirea and senecio in front of dahlias, asters and helianthus. The colours, too, are pale blues and yellows at the ends of the borders, rising to a climax of red *Papaver orientalis* and orange day lilies in the centre.

Open on selected afternoons and by appointment. Tel: 0256 862827.

PENSHURST PLACE

Kent

TONBRIDGE

*A*lthough there has been a garden at Penshurst Place, in the Weald of Kent, since the 14th century, the layout that we see today was largely determined in the time of the first Elizabeth. In the 1550s Sir Henry Sidney moved thousands of tons of soil to build a great parterre to the south of the house, 360ft (110m) by 300ft (91m), retained by walls and terraces. During the family's decline in the 18th and 19th centuries this structure was left broadly intact, and the present owner's great grandfather, the 2nd Lord De L'Isle and Dudley, created the magnificent Italian garden on the Elizabethan parterre and planted the yew hedges which are so much a feature of Penshurst. The late Viscount De L'Isle, who came to the house in 1945, restored the gardens so

Below left, warm colours predominate in the beds below the fruit trees

Below right, a stunning display of red and white roses

first, four beds of *Rosa* 'King Arthur' are edged with red berberis and *R.* 'Elizabeth of Glamis' with lavender. Among the standard roses are 'Iceberg', 'Etoile de Holland' and 'Mischief', and beneath them the velvety *Stachys lanata*. In the Spring and Autumn Garden, rows of nut trees are underplanted with daffodils and tulips for stunning spring colour, to be followed later on by the warm colours of hardy fuchsias and spire lilies.

Between these two layouts is the Middle Walk, designed as a shrub border by the late Lanning Roper, with the bright reds and yellows of senecio, cotinus, phlomis and *Sedum spectabile*, and in the end hedge there is a 'window' matched by a squint in the house. The Italian parterre centres on an oval fountain surrounded with

that, today, they are a feast of colour set within a firm, architectural framework.

On entering the garden from the car park you see the splendid, double herbaceous border backed by yew and overhung with apple trees. Flag irises, anemones, achilleas, hemerocallis, lilies and astilbes welcome you with their seasonal colour, while beyond the hedge are the Rose Garden and the Spring and Autumn Garden. In the

dwarf box hedges enclosing 'Elizabeth Arden' roses, and the terrace walls are draped with 'New Dawn' and 'Queen Elizabeth'.

The Tudor Terrace is planted with red acers, while the Nut Garden has coppiced Kentish cobnuts and four avenues of crab apples lushly underplanted with a mixture of miniature daffodils, bluebells, primroses, tulips and cowslips. An Inner Pergola, covered with wisteria,

honeysuckle and climbing roses, stands romantically in the middle. Halfway down the Yew Alley is Diana's Bath, a lily pond where water hyacinths and aponogeton flourish. To the south is the attractive Grey Garden, created by John Codrington, which is full of delicate artemisias and dianthus beneath the willow-leaved pear. The Theatre Garden, once the drying ground, is covered in yellow and white tulips which give way to lacecap hydrangeas in summer, while, alongside, the Magnolia Garden boasts a particularly fine *Magnolia x soulangiana*. A recent addition is the Flag Garden, which represents the pattern of the Union Jack. In spring there are red and white tulips, followed by roses with blue and white lavender.

Open from March to October, daily except Monday. Tel: 0892 870304 or 870307.

A frothy pink rose adorns the gateway

SISSINGHURST CASTLE GARDEN
Kent

SISSINGHURST, 2 MILES (3 KM) NORTH-EAST OF CRANBROOK

All established gardens have a strong sense of their own history, and nowhere is this notion of 'place' stronger than at Sissinghurst Castle. Probably one of the best known and admired gardens in the world, it is not only the breathtaking beauty of its White Garden, the Lime Walk and the Rose Garden that separately constitute its attraction, but its coherent development from 12th-century moated manor house, through Elizabethan mansion, to the romantic brick tower restored by Vita Sackville-West and her husband, Sir Harold Nicolson, and the wonderful garden that they created, which gives it its special character.

with box and a circular lawn, with roses trained over the central roundel. Vita Sackville-West loved old-fashioned roses, and here there are 'Fantin-Latour', 'Charles de Mills', Camaieux' and 'Gloire de Dijon' to be seen. Beyond this colourful garden is the Lime Walk, with its long borders filled in spring with grape hyacinths, tulips, fritillaries, narcissi and anemones, backed by an avenue of pleached limes. The Cottage Garden has a colour scheme predominantly orange, red and gold, with euphorbias, polyanthus and trollius, as well as poppies, tree peonies and the yellow-green of *Hosta fortunei* 'Aurea'. Beyond the Moat Walk, blooming with wallflowers in summer, is the Nuttery,

Far left, tawny wallflowers and creamy peonies set the colour scheme for the Cottage Garden

Left, purple nemesia spills from a stone trough

The design of the garden is Harold Nicolson's; the planting Vita Sackville-West's, and in contrast to the linear, classical layout, the plants were encouraged to spill out over the paths and the wildflowers to set seed. The Tower Courtyard has four Irish yews underplanted with violets in spring, and rosemary 'Sissinghurst Blue' is on either side of the tower arch. Against the red Tudor brick the rose 'Allen Chandler' grows, as does a flowering quince, and there is also a trough of blue columbines. *Magnolia grandiflora* stretches upwards, with a ceanothus and the Chilean potato tree. Running to the east of the library is the Purple Border, planted with annual and perennial shrubs in shades of blue, mauve and purple. On the opposite side of the courtyard *Hydrangea petiolaris* stands above the archway, and a viburnum is trained up the wall with aquilegias planted below.

The Rose Garden has beds edged

and further on again, the Herb Garden surrounded by yew hedges. The Orchard, stretching down to the moat, is bright with daffodils and flowering cherries in the spring, and boasts *Rosa gallica* 'Sissinghurst Castle', an ancient variety rediscovered in 1930.

Entry to the White Garden is to the north of the formal Yew Walk, and it needs little introduction. Box hedges frame the beds which Vita Sackville-West planted in white and silver. Here, lilies, delphiniums, galtonia and speedwell, a central white rose surrounded by spiraea, pulmonaria and *Peonia* 'Ivory Jewel' spread their magic, while a weeping pear stands sentinel beside a slender lead statue of a virgin. With white wisteria covering the wall behind the pergola, there seems little more to be said about a garden of such beauty, except: 'Go and see it for yourself!'

Open from April to mid-October, most afternoons. Tel: 0580 712850.

Rhododendrons and azaleas colour the woodland without dominating it

SPINNERS
Hampshire

BOLDRE, 1 MILE (1.5 KM) NORTH-EAST OF LYMINGTON

Standing on a wooded slope falling westward towards the Lymington River, Spinners is a garden where the spirit of the New Forest has been jealously preserved. Although it is only 2 acres (1ha) in extent, it is full of interesting and beautiful plants, particularly those that like shady conditions. Part of the garden is sheltered by a canopy of oaks, but the layout also includes an open space and a fine lawn below the house. Numerous winding paths traverse the woodland, with glades charmingly opening up at intervals.

Rhododendrons and azaleas permeate but do not dominate the woodland. In spring a fine *Rhododendron Loderi* 'King George' shows its dark pink buds, while near by you can see *R. davidsonianum*, a triflorum with flowers that range from pink to lilac-mauve. Camellias also feature – particularly the *williamsii* hybrids – as do magnolias and lacecap and mophead hydrangeas. There are a number of species of dogwoods, and Japanese maples are plentiful, especially the bright pink *Acer palmatum* 'Chisio Improved'. In spring the ground beneath the trees is thickly carpeted with flowers, including violets, periwinkles, erythroniums, anemones, bloodroot and lungwort. Later in the summer hostas and lilies take over, supported by euphorbias, particularly *E. griffithii* 'Fireglow'.

In a clearing below the steep woodland slope, fringed bleeding heart, with its blue-green leaves, is set against a berberis, while near by there are trilliums, hellebores and pulmonaria. Cranesbill geraniums are another speciality, and in a boggy area close by ostrich ferns and periwinkles flourish. The stone path that runs behind the house leads to an area with tree peonies, euphorbias, day lilies and lady's smock. Above the plant sales area there is a small path which runs among many varieties of erythroniums and passes a small example of *Rhododendron roxieanum orearastes*, which has glossy, narrow leaves and creamy flowers. To the south of the nursery is an open area where two outstanding magnolias can be seen, *Magnolia x loebneri* 'Leonard Messel', with lilac-pink flowers, and 'Merrill', which has white flowers. Although Spinners is a small garden, it has much to interest and delight the plant lover.

Open daily from mid-April to August, and by appointment. Tel: 0590 673347.

A wide variety of planting is packed into this small country garden, inluding many shade-lovers (left), and cranesbill geraniums (above)

STREET HOUSE
Surrey

THURSLEY, 5 MILES (8 KM) SOUTH-WEST OF GODALMING

The deep Surrey countryside boasts many gardens both large and small, but few can match the important historical associations and charm of Street House, at Thursley, between Milford and Hindhead. In the fine Regency house the great architect Sir Edwin Lutyens spent his early and most formative years, and it was while he was designing Crooksbury, his first commission, in this house that he met Gertrude Jekyll, who was to have such a lasting influence both on him and on the design of the great ensemble of Edwardian country house and garden epitomised by their unique partnership.

The attractive 1827 house stands behind a row of imposing lime trees underplanted with lady's mantle, and as you turn the corner of the building to enter the 1½ acre (0.5ha) garden, a glance behind reveals a view of the village church framed by three sycamore trees. It soon becomes apparent that there are three separate gardens at Street House. At the back, a curved island bed in the centre of a spacious lawn spills over with purple delphiniums, white foxgloves and lupins, underplanted with *Stachys lanata* and *Alchemilla mollis*.

Below this, on the mezzanine level, is a circular astrological mandala, incorporating a small round pond. It was built by the present owner, Mrs B M Francis, in local ironstone and Bargate stone unearthed from the garden. Near by, in the Lower Garden, in a secluded corner edged by artemisias and *Lonicera nitida* 'Baggesen's Gold', is a wooden seat designed by Lutyens, and a short flight of stone steps brings you past a spiky verbascum to the main lawn at the side of the house. The walled garden is full of unusual and interesting plants, trees and shrubs, including *Rubus x tridel*, the thornless shrub with peeling bark which produces white, rose-like flowers in early summer, and a great acacia, *Robinia pseudoacacia*.

Street House boasts a magnificent *Cornus kousa*, a Japanese snowball tree, some rare old-fashioned roses including *Rosa mundi*, and 'Cardinal Richelieu', 'Blue Diamond' rhododendrons and camellias. From the gardens there is also a wonderful view towards the Devil's Punch Bowl, one of Surrey's most famous beauty spots.

Open on selected days during the summer.

Above, signs in the stonework of the astrological mandala

Left, a charmingly overgrown path

Far left, a view across the garden to the village church

COTTESBROOKE HALL
Northamptonshire

COTTESBROOKE, 9 MILES (14.5 KM) NORTH-WEST OF NORTHAMPTON

Great cedars of Lebanon offer shelter to the borders on the terrace

To the north of Northampton, in that secluded countryside which saw the Civil War battle of Naseby, is the early 18th-century Cottesbrooke Hall. Thought to be the model used by Jane Austen for *Mansfield Park*, the lovely house and its surrounding gardens are approached over the classical Mitchell Bridge. The splendid parkland was also created at the same time, but by an unknown hand, and the more formal layout and the Wild Garden were devised by Edward Schultz, Sir Geoffrey Jellicoe and Dame Sylvia Crowe, though inspired by the late Hon. Lady Macdonald-Buchanan. The result is a series of charming enclosed courtyards and gardens around the house, immaculately maintained by the present owners, Captain and Mrs J Macdonald-Buchanan, and their head gardener, Mrs Daw.

On entering the garden opposite the west wing, there is a magnificent view of the lake and of Brixworth Church,

which dates originally from Anglo Saxon times. A large tulip tree, an *Acer griseum* and several magnolias can be seen, while the forecourt to the garden in front of the house has large vases planted with rhododendrons and agapanthus. Beyond the wrought-iron gates and two rose beds is the Statue Walk, with Peter Scheemakers's four statues from the Temple of Ancient Virtue, at Stowe, backed by clipped yews and facing a herbaceous border, while on either side of Eagle Gates are further borders with large wisterias and a fragrant pineapple-scented Moroccan broom. To the east is the Dilemma Garden with, between its 'horns', old roses, a fastigiate tulip tree, a golden Indian bean, a pocket handkerchief tree and an old mulberry. Opposite is the Pool Garden with some fine magnolias, a large

Carpentaria californica with its glossy dark green foliage, ceanothus and a lovely *Actinidia kolomikta*.

An overflowing urn stands before the pergola

In the Dutch Garden, with its two sundials, there is spectacular spring and summer bedding within miniature box hedges, while the Pine Court alongside is dominated by an old Scots pine with a climbing hydrangea. The terrace has extensive herbaceous borders with a wonderful display of foliage plants, including yuccas and euphorbias, partly sheltered by ancient cedars of Lebanon.

In early May the Spinney Garden shines with brightly coloured bulbs and azaleas, a snakebark maple, a Tibetan cherry, a Judas tree, and weeping beeches. Beyond a thatched Wendy house, a small stream flows beside two wild gardens planted with azaleas, rhododendrons, primroses and daffodils. Hostas, hellebores, ligularias and astilbes grow in profusion by the bridge, and there is also a bank of bamboos in front of the so-called Japanese yew.

Open from April to September, on one afternoon a week and some bank holidays. Tel: 060 124 808.

CROSSING HOUSE
Cambridgeshire

SHEPRETH, 8 MILES (13 KM) SOUTH OF CAMBRIDGE

Although Crossing House has a small garden, there are more than 5000 species to be seen and the greenhouses are packed with unusual plants. It must also be one of the best known of country gardens, as it stands alongside the level crossing at Shepreth on the busy Cambridge-to-Royston railway line. The beauty of the garden, cultivated by Mr and Mrs Douglas Fuller over the past 30 years, and the half mile of railway embankment that they also care for, must have raised the spirits of many a traveller on this railway line.

As a conscious decision, the owners have decided to ensure that the visitor has something of interest to see whatever the time of year. Plant experts have identified 35 varieties of snowdrop at Crossing House, giant forms and those with green and yellow tips, while early spring produces drifts of naturalised crocuses, including *Crocus tommasinianus* 'Whitewell Purple', and many varieties of scillas. These are replaced as the season progresses by alliums, hardy terrestrial orchids like *Dactylorrhiza foliosa*, with its spikes of bright purple or pink flowers, Shirley poppies and flax.

Clematis provides summer colour, and there are many varieties of roses, some of them fragrant. Raised limestone beds hold alpines. During the autumn, Japanese anemones, colchicums and schizostylis, and the Kaffir lily are eye-catching, especially 'Viscountess Byng' with its pink flowers. Even in winter there is much to see, as rare hellebores, early crocus and irises are in flower during a mild period, as are viburnums and winter jasmine.

Although the soil at Shepreth is alkaline, rhododendrons, azaleas and pernettyas have been planted in containers of lime-free compost, and several varieties of Asiatic gentians are also grown in a trough. Two ponds have been added to the layout, and one has become a haven for wildlife, with frogs, toads and newts in residence. One of the three greenhouses is stocked with alpines, lewisias being strongly represented, while the others hold South African bulbs, many of them grown from seed, and also leptospermum, especially 'Burgundy Queen' with its dark-red flowers, and 'Keatleys', which is pink. It is surely remarkable what can be achieved in a small space in this country garden, from the dwarf box-edging to beds, to great yew arches, and the beauty of the scene must give encouragement to us all.

Open daily throughout the year. Tel: 0763 261071.

Left, an inspiration to commuters, the Crossing House shows just what can be done with a small garden

Above, the garden extends along the trackside – though this part is out of bounds to visitors

ELTON HALL
Cambridgeshire

8 MILES (13 KM) WEST OF PETERBOROUGH

Just to the west of Peterborough, in the gently undulating countryside that stretches towards Oundle and Rockingham Forest, is the fine estate of Elton Hall. There has been a house on the site since the Norman Conquest, and the family of the present owners, Mr and Mrs William Proby, have lived there for 300 years. Such continuity is apparent not only in

Perfect blooms in the rose garden

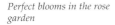

'rooms' and to provide a magnificent backdrop to the knot herb garden and statuary. The Victorian Rose Garden is now a delight, not least because of the scent of the 1000 roses that drifts upwards on a still, hot day in July, and because of the interest of the many old-fashioned varieties that can be seen. 'Mutabilis' stands alongside the white and blush-pink flowers of the

the building itself, which, though constructed in the main from the 17th century, incorporates the Sapcote Tower and a chapel, both dating from about 1485, but also in the gardens, which were laid out between 1909 and 1911. When Mr and Mrs Proby came to Elton in 1979 the gardens were in a very poor state, and a programme of clearance had to be undertaken before restoration could begin. It is a tribute to their determination and plantsmanship that the gardens now provide a worthy setting for such a splendid house.

In order to re-establish the bones of the Edwardian layout hedges have been planted mainly in yew and in hornbeam to separate the different upright Bourbon, 'Boule de Neige', while 'Gruss en Aachen', *Rosa mundi* and 'Sander's White Rambler' can also be seen.

In the middle of the lovely Sunken Garden there is a lily pond, and the borders are bright in summer with an unusual selection of foliage and flowering plants, among them *Papaver orientale* 'Mrs Perry', peonies, *Philadelphus* 'Manteau d'Hermine' with its fragrant creamy-white flowers, and with *Crambe cordifolia*. The Shrub Garden shows *Viburnum opulus* 'Compactum' with its profuse white flowers, smooth sumach, the bottlebrush buckeye underplanted with hostas, and *Hydrangea arborescens*, while the herbaceous border below the Sapcote Tower is about to be replanted with a blue and yellow colour scheme. The deep border along the terrace now has pink and silver plants, and includes some roses, while clematis climbs up the walls.

A recent project has been the planting of an arboretum which includes *Keaki zelkova serrata*, evergreen oak, *Paulownia tomentosa*, the foxglove tree, the dawn redwood and *Fagus sylvatica* 'Dawyck Purple', which has erect branches. The restoration of this 8 acre (3ha) garden is a welcome initiative, that will appeal both to the plant lover and to those who just appreciate a beautiful setting.

Open from Easter to August, on selected afternoons.

A profusion of old-fashioned roses in red, white and all shades of pink

HADDON HALL
Derbyshire

2 MILES (3 KM) SOUTH-EAST OF BAKEWELL

Perched high above the River Wye on a limestone escarpment, Haddon Hall is one of the most romantic medieval castles in England. The grey and honey colour of its stonework is a sharp contrast to the rich green of the woodland behind, and beautiful gardens spill down in a series of walled terraces from Dorothy Vernon's door at the very top of the bowling alley. When the 9th Duke of Rutland restored Haddon in 1912, he cleared this terrace of giant yews, as well as sycamores and ivy on the walls. Pairs of clipped yew trees are again a feature of this garden which, in the spring, glows with more than 60 varieties of daffodils, polyanthus and wallflowers. As summer approaches, the roses take

The fountain terrace, with its beds of roses and lavender, and the Elizabethan border below the gallery windows

castle almost to the level of the river itself. Tradition has it that Haddon came into the hands of the Dukes of Rutland when the Vernon heiress eloped with John Manners, son of the then Earl of Rutland, in the 1560s, running down the 76 drystone steps and across the packhorse bridge to meet her lover.

Whatever the truth of the story, the steps from Dorothy Vernon's door, which is the route by which the modern visitor leaves the house, descend to a terrace which was once a over: first the climbers, including *Rosa primula*, the incense rose, and then the floribundas and the hybrid teas in the formal beds. Haddon also boasts a collection of clematis, with 'Mrs Cholmondley' showing large, blue blooms in early summer beside the upper door.

A wide flight of steps leads down to the Fountain Terrace which lies beneath the irregular window panes of the magnificent Jacobean long gallery. A simple, rectangular pool with its delicate jet of water contrasts with the

surrounding lawn and the beds that show favourites such as 'King's Ransom' and 'Wendy Cussons', while the gallery wall itself is covered with a variety of climbing roses coloured pink, yellow and deep red. Beneath this magnificent display is an Elizabethan border, with native plants and those introduced during the 16th century – aquilegias, dame's violet and love-lies-bleeding, while, further along, is a bed with more than 30 varieties of delphiniums that make a splendid display in early July.

From the end of Fountain Terrace there are spectacular views over the Wye and the surrounding countryside. Although the lower terraces are not open to the public, the retaining walls harbour a wide range of rock plants which create a colourful patchwork during the spring, raising the question of whether the medieval lords of Haddon planted a series of gardens in these defensive terraces the equal of those we so admire today.

Open from Easter to September, on selected days. Tel: 0629 812855.

Part of the display of over 30 varieties of delphiniums

❃

HELMINGHAM HALL
Suffolk

STOWMARKET, 9 MILES (14.5 KM) NORTH-EAST OF IPSWICH

❃

A mauvy-blue delphinium from the herbaceous border

Helmingham Hall is the home of the ancient Tollemache family. Standing serenely inside its deep moat, the mellow brickwork of the Tudor house is appropriately surrounded by a magnificent garden centred on a 19th-century parterre. This is edged with a beautiful spring border which leads into a lushly planted enclosure on the site of the old kitchen garden. Beyond this again is an orchard and apple walk; on the other side of the house is a historical knot and herb garden designed in 1982 for the Tollemaches by Lady Salisbury.

Entering the main gardens along a grassy causeway which runs between the house moat and the one which surrounds the parterre, you come at once to a rose garden filled with hybrid musks. Here, the familiar 'Penelope', 'Felicia', 'Pink Prosperity' and 'Buff Beauty' bloom alongside rarer varieties such as 'Danae', 'Daybreak' and 'Nur Mahal', and there are also American ones such as 'Bishop Darlington'. This part of the garden is

Vegetables still grow behind the colourful borders in the old kitchen garden

a wide rectangle with classical stone figures at each end, the banks dotted with primroses and narcissi in spring. The roses themselves grow in wide beds edged with Hidcote lavender and underplanted with London pride, which provides a carpet through which peonies, *Campanula latiflora* and alstroemeria also grow.

Through the gates of the walled garden, a central grassy path divides the area into eight beds, as it did when this was an Elizabethan kitchen garden. Bordered by herbaceous plants and backed by climbing roses, among them 'Albertine' and 'New Dawn', the vegetable plots are divided by walks and arched tunnels on which sweetpeas, gourds and runner beans grow. The main herbaceous borders are immensely colourful with acanthus, alliums, delphiniums, achillea and *Papaver orientalis*, while the Orchard Garden in spring is covered with primroses, cowslips, wild orchids and ox-eye daisies. The low box hedges of the knot to the east of the house contain herbs. There is also a magnificent collection of shrub roses mixed with campanulas, geraniums, foxgloves and lady's mantle. Enclosed by yew hedges, this is a beautiful garden where all the plants have been chosen to be contemporary with the house.

Open from May to September, on most Sunday afternoons. Tel: 0473 890217.

Winged horse-heads stand proudly on the gate pillars of the walled garden

ILMINGTON MANOR
Warwickshire

ILMINGTON, 4 MILES (6.5 KM) NORTH-WEST OF SHIPSTON-ON-STOUR

The sundial, adrift in a sea of gentle grey foliage and soft pink roses

Few who visit the lovely gardens of Ilmington Manor today would guess that they are only 70 years old. When the late Mr Spenser Flower came to this magical village in 1919, the honey-coloured stone manor house dating from 1600 had become a place for squatters, and an orchard occupied the position of the present garden. With a flair for design and with a clear idea of what he wanted, Mr Flower restored and enlarged his new home, and then, with the help of his wife, who was a keen plantswoman, set about creating the interesting and beautiful garden that we see today.

To the right of the drive, which is lined with hornbeams, is a little Pond Garden. The edges of the tank itself were decorated with carved stone panels that Mr Flower had found and considered to be Jacobean, and the surrounding paving is overgrown with many different varieties of scented thyme. The beds are filled with pink diascea, dianthus and other sun-lovers, while trailing sedums continue the patterns on the walls of the pool. This attractive area is bounded to the north and east by walls draped with clematis, a fine banksia rose and other aromatic climbers, but it is a surprise to find *Buddleia crispa*, as this has a reputation for tenderness.

The Pillar Borders are separated by a grass walk and present a most unusual combination of shrubs and herbaceous plants carefully arranged in colour groups.

Steps lead into the formal Rose Garden, among two long borders planted with old and modern shrub

Ilmington Manor – although this is really more of an informal cottage garden. Designed by the present owner, Mr D Flower's cousin, Lady Flower, it features the most enchanting mixture of roses, lavender and scented mock oranges, and peonies and hardy geraniums stand alongside clematis-

roses. 'Madame Hardy' and 'Scarlet Fire' can be seen, as can 'Louise Odier', 'Cerise Bouquet' and 'Charles de Mills', while there are modern long-flowering specimens such as 'Arthur Bell' and 'Scented Air'. Beyond three large walnut trees and a dovecote perched high above a neatly clipped hedge are drifts of naturalised daffodils and brightly coloured crocuses in spring. A low, circular rock garden built of local limestone partly encloses the orchard, and the other side is flanked by imposing shrubs and beautiful herbaceous plants.

The so-called Dutch Garden is in one of the most colourful parts of

clad walls. Large varieties of lily such as *Lilium regale* and *L. speciosum rubrum* make a dramatic appearance, while hemerocallis and agapanthus grow together. In Lady Flower's White Border artemisias and senecios compete with white penstemons and variegated laurustinus. Although the design of this garden must have been influenced by Lawrence Johnston's Hidcote (see page 38), which is only a few miles away, it is very individual, and will give constant pleasure and delight however often it is visited.

Open on selected days from May to July, and by appointment. Tel: 060 882 230.

A corner of the colourful Dutch Garden

MANNINGTON HALL GARDENS
Norfolk

SAXTHORPE, 18 MILES (29 KM) NORTH-WEST OF NORWICH

Only 7 miles (11 km) from the sea in the open, rolling countryside of North Norfolk is the romantic Mannington Hall. Purchased in the 18th century by the brother of Sir Robert Walpole, the lovely medieval moated house is still owned by the Walpole family. Although the gardens are being extended, there are a number of areas to interest the garden lover, especially the Heritage Rose Garden – a deliciously scented layout – and a wild valley planted with unusual trees.

Walking across the spacious lawns towards the house, it is clear that the recent storms have badly damaged some of the great cedars, but fast-growing wellingtonias have been planted to replace those lost. Inside the Victorian 'battlement' walls, the borders are overflowing with herbaceous plants and roses, with *Rosa* 'Canary Bird' showing its

The exuberant architecture of Mannington Hall makes a fine background for its celebrated collection of roses

single yellow blooms in late spring. The bed beneath the house wall has peonies and lupins, while on the wall itself is a fine climbing hydrangea, *H. petiolaris*, and opposite is a splendid weeping pear with grey-green leaves.

Around the corner of the house *Rosa banksiae* 'Lutea' climbs vigorously close to a mauve wisteria, while rock roses brighten up the gravel with their pink and white flowers in early summer. A formal rose garden dominated by hybrid teas and with a sundial in the centre is surrounded by juniper. Within the moat an intricate pattern of sweetly scented herbs are planted underneath urns, filled with hyacinths in spring and replaced by brightly coloured pelargoniums later on.

Fruit trees line the intimate enclosure of the Heritage Rose Garden, which is divided into several areas, each representing a period of the rose's historical development. In all there are more than 1000 different varieties, including a wide range of wild roses. The Medieval Garden has turf seats and some very old roses, including *Rosa gallica* 'officianalis', and *R. spinosissima* stand near a small yew tree. Beyond the other formal areas of Mannington Hall, which include a tranquil 17th-century knot garden, is a spectacular wild valley. Here, in a totally different mood, there are many fascinating trees, including seven specimens of *Acer palmatum* which are well over 100 years old.

Open from Easter to October, on Sunday afternoons. Tel: 026 387 284

Norsth of Grantham and close to the busy A1 lies the secluded oasis of Marston Hall. A number of small gardens and courtyards flanked by walls and high hedges surround the ancient house built of Ancaster stone, creating a setting which is at once wholly consistent with and redolent of the medieval period in which Marston Hall was originally built. Although today owned by the Reverend Henry Thorold, a cousin of the 15th baronet, Sir Anthony Thorold, Marston Hall used to be the principal seat of one of the oldest families in Lincolnshire.

From the drive up to the 3 acre (1ha) garden you can see one of the largest wych elms in the country standing opposite the main door of the house. Approximately 12ft (3.5m) in diameter, it is perhaps 400 years old, and, in spite of having been attacked by Dutch elm disease, it is now putting out new shoots. Just as remarkable is the great laburnum, in the Shrubbery Walk, close to the entrance to the churchyard, which is thought to be one of the largest in England and was planted in the late 16th century.

To the south of the house is a splendid rose garden, enclosed by yew hedges, and with climbers draped on wooden pyramids in the traditional manner, and old-fashioned roses as well as modern varieties planted in formal beds. Beyond this is a secluded area, with hedges surrounding herbaceous borders and vegetables, and a Gothick gazebo decorated with murals by Barbara Jones. A knot garden is filled with herbs, among them rosemary, thyme and mints, and beyond the lawns there are romantic walks through the newly planted Laburnum Avenue.

To mark the Reverend Thorold's retirement from the staff of Lancing College, the Lancing Avenue of Lombardy poplars has been planted. It stretches from the orchard westward to the River Witham near by, achieving a perfect synthesis between the formal layout of the garden and the parkland beyond. In every respect, Marston Hall evokes the history of this part of Lincolnshire and of the families that have lived there for many centuries.

Open on selected afternoons and by appointment.

MARSTON HALL
Lincolnshire

MARSTON, 6 MILES (9.5 KM) NORTH OF GRANTHAM

Above, pyramids of wooden trellis stand in the rose garden, an elegant architectural feature in their own right

Left, a tranquil corner

MOSELEY OLD HALL
Staffordshire

3½ MILES (5.5 KM) NORTH OF WOLVERHAMPTON

*I*n one of the least promising parts of Wolverhampton you suddenly come upon the truly remarkable Moseley Old Hall, set in its equally amazing garden. From the outside, the house belies its age, but as soon as you enter it is clear that this is a timber-framed Tudor manor house – and indeed, it is the building in which the future Charles II took refuge after his defeat at the Battle of Worcester in 1651. When the property was given to the National Trust in 1962 it was in a bad condition, and the 1 acre (0.5ha) garden was virtually non-existent. Within a very short time, however, Graham Stuart Thomas, assisted by Miles Hadfield, had recreated the garden in the mid-17th-century style,

An excellent view of the formal knot garden, with its trimmed trees and neatly raked gravel

which, now fully matured, forms the wonderful layout we see today.

The main feature of the garden is the knot which lies to the south of the Hall and is best seen from its upper windows. A copy of one designed by the Reverend Walter Stonehouse in 1640, it consists of 11 clipped spheres of box standing on 3ft (1m) stems surrounded by circular gravel beds edged with dwarf box hedges. Along one side of the knot is an arbour now draped with the fragrant *Clematis flammula*, the white-flowering virgin's bower, and *Clematis viticella*, making a contrast with the deep-purple Teinturier grape, while narrow borders are filled with strongly scented lavender.

The arbour leads through a hornbeam tunnel to the Nut Alley, lined on each side with different varieties of snowdrops, winter aconites and the Siberian squill flower in early spring. These are succeeded by the stinking hellebores and by snake's head fritillary, followed in autumn by colchicums and pink-flowering cyclamens. At the end of the alley is the gate through which Charles Stuart is supposed to have entered secretly, and in the field beyond is one sweet chestnut, all that remains from the Long Walk. The flagged path leading to the back door is lined with morello cherries, quinces, black mulberries and medlars. At the far end is a small herb garden enclosed by box, with a fragrant mock orange underplanted with Lenten roses.

The front garden, once a paved court, now consists of lawns with spirals and cones of box, and two beds of tutsan edged by *Teucrium chamaedrys*. The mixed borders against the walls are filled with splendid herbs like Solomon's seal, red valerian, the pink and white varieties of *Paeonia officianalis*, and the lovely garden herb soapwort, the soapy sap of which is nowadays used in museums for laundering and revitalising precious fabrics. Moseley Old Hall is an enchanting garden, full of interesting plants that were once grown for medicinal and cleaning purposes and to provide dyes.

Open on selected days from April to October. Tel: 0902 782808.

In complete contrast, an informal flower border is set against the old wall

NETHERFIELD HERBS
Suffolk

ROUGHAM, 4½ MILES (6.5 KM) EAST OF BURY ST EDMUNDS

Grassy paths lead between the neat box-edged beds

Set deep in the Suffolk countryside near Bury St Edmunds is a small but very distinguished herb garden, Netherfield Herbs. The owner, Lesley Bremness, has been growing herbs and writing about them now for more than 20 years, and a visit to Netherfield undoubtedly deepens one's knowledge about the many uses to which herbs can be put – in cooking, in medicinal remedies and in cosmetics.

As soon as you enter there is a small enclosure which contains two cartwheels, one planted with many varieties of thyme, and the other spilling over with mint, the spokes making a natural division. Around the edges of the courtyard are more herbs, all carefully labelled, revealing, for instance, that lovage as an antiseptic can be applied to wounds, the roots of the musk mallow can cure coughs and urinary complaints, while parsley is rich in vitamins A, B and C. Beyond the 16th-century thatched cottage are two attractive box-edged knot gardens, the subtle foliage colours being provided by the silver curry plant, *Helichrysum augustifolium*, pale green santolina and the shiny evergreen leaves of teucrium.

Four demonstration beds in the centre of the densely planted herb garden are devoted to sages, rosemaries, oreganos, marjorams and

A great variety of herbs, for culinary and medicinal use, are grown here

thymes. The prostrate sage keeps its leaves late into the year, but the pineapple sage needs to be overwintered indoors. *Akebia quinata*, a hardy semi-evergreen, covers an arbour seat, and as well as being deliciously fragrant the tiny, purple-red flowers of this elegant climber turn into edible fruits if the summer has been a hot one. Near by is a pale pink, highly scented damask rose, the petals of which are used for rose oil and rosewater, while the tiny sweet briar, full of apple fragrance, stands over apricot-coloured foxgloves.

In one corner a golden hop is trained on to a cherry, underplanted with elecampane, the aromatic root of which Helen of Troy was supposed to have been collecting when she was abducted by Paris. Two 16th-century beds contain salad herbs – purslane and salad rocket – and medicinal herbs including blue and pink comfrey. A small statue of Pan beneath a weeping pear is surrounded by white and crimson roses, and there are also many culinary herbs to be found, including sweet cicely, tansy, broad-leaved sorrel and bible herb. This most enchanting garden does much to correct the general ignorance about these useful plants as well as giving pleasure to all with its scent and beauty.

Open daily.

NEWSTEAD ABBEY
Nottinghamshire

LINBY

*A*lthough associated with the name of the poet, Lord Byron, Newstead Abbey has a long and distinguished history in which its gardens play an appropriately important part. Founded by Henry II as a priory in the 12th century, Newstead was acquired by Sir John Byron of Colwick at the dissolution of the monasteries, and the 5th Lord Byron, as well as being tried for murder and acquitted, was responsible for adding the Upper Lake to the 25 acres (10ha) of gardens, which came into the hands of Nottingham-shire County Council on presentation by the last owner, Sir Julian Caln, in the 1930s.

From the entry to the 300 acre (120ha) estate alongside the so-called Gospel Oak, the long drive sweeps through rhododendron plantations that date from the last century, and crosses open heathland covered with heather to reach a car park to the north of the abbey. Water flows over a cascade into the Garden Lake, and the walls of the house are festooned with jasmine and the fragrant yellow rose 'Golden Showers'. Close to the east wall is the Spanish Garden, named after an Iberian well-head which is its centrepiece. This gives on to a gravel path bounded by a wall covered with hydrangeas and honeysuckles, its border filled with shade-loving plants. A pocket handkerchief tree marks the entry to a dark, dank tunnel which leads to Eagle Pond, one of the monks' original stew ponds. Just to the west is the famous memorial to Boatswain, Byron's dog, and the wood

Swathes of roses, ancient and modern, adorn the former kitchen garden

beyond is planted with snowdrops
and daffodils which make a brave
show in spring.

In the former kitchen garden beds
at each end display old-fashioned
roses, while modern roses are set in
beds surrounded by lawns, and
climbers and ramblers adorn the walls
of the enclosure. Beyond the great
Yew Walk is a fine rock garden and
also the famous Japanese Garden
commissioned by Miss Ethel Webb,
whose family owned Newstead in the
early years of this century. Hump-
backed bridges and stepping stones
across the streams lead between
rhododendrons, azaleas, mahonias,
skimmias and bamboo. Returning to
the Garden Lake, you can enjoy the
beauty of a pergola covered with roses
and other climbers, and what is
probably the best view of the abbey in
this extensive and beautiful garden.

Open daily. Tel: 0623 793557.

*Bridges and stepping stones
show the way through the
famous Japanese Garden*

SHERBOURNE PARK
Warwickshire

SHERBOURNE, 3 MILES (5 KM) SOUTH OF WARWICK

Above, a section of the parterre

Right above, the church is drawn into the garden, domminating the view

Right below, the charming red-brick house, which pre- dates the garden by nearly 100 years

*I*t has long been a tradition of English garden-making that the layout should respond to, and draw its inspiration from, its countryside setting. Nowhere is this consistency more apparent than in the lovely gardens of Sherbourne Park. Set deep in lush countryside with fine views over farmland to the River Avon, and adjacent to Sherbourne Church – built in 1863 by Sir George Gilbert Scott – the red-brick house was built in early Georgian times by Smith of Warwick.

When the Smith-Rylands came to live at Sherbourne Park in 1953 there was little in the way of a garden, and one of the first steps was to create a ha-ha to protect the garden from straying cattle while preserving the views, not least the one of the new avenue of poplars, centred on the house but planted outside the ditch. The tall tower of the church has almost been incorporated into the garden too, as it dominates the views over the L-shaped lake from the main terrace and from the Bottom Garden. The construction of a swimming pool on the south side of the house in 1960 prompted the creation of a series of beautiful 'garden rooms' by the designer of the layout, Lady Smith-Ryland.

Immediately outside the house a paved terrace is now covered by clematis, wisteria and a *Magnolia grandiflora*, with fuchsias growing in terracotta pots. The pool pavilion gives shelter to a border which boasts

Mahonia x media 'Charity', and, inside the enclosure itself, beds contain honeysuckle, agapanthus, nerines and an old rose, 'Bennett's Seedling', trained on the wall. Down a flight of steps is the Bottom Garden, planted like an orchard except that the trees are sorbus. The far end of this area is screened by golden and green yews into which *Rosa longicuspis* and 'Paul's Himalayan Musk' have been allowed to climb. A simple parterre has been created close to the churchyard wall, the beds edged with box and filled with roses, grey-leaved herbs and perennials, with honeysuckle in the corners.

The White Garden is surrounded by yew hedges with four *Juniperus virginiana* 'Skyrocket' dominating the central bed, while other borders contain philadelphus, rock roses, lychnis, delphiniums, geraniums and anthemis. Beyond, there is a way through a garden with a group of weeping pears to an arboretum with ailanthus, beeches, whitebeam, *Salix matsudana* and *Cedrus deodara*. There is yet another garden to the east of the house and that too reinforces the link, so apparent at Sherbourne Park, between the garden and the surrounding countryside.

Open on selected afternoons and by appointment. Tel: 0926 624255.

BODNANT GARDEN
Gwynedd

TAL-Y-CAFN, 8 MILES (13 KM) SOUTH OF LLANDUDNO

Set high above the River Conwy with spectacular views over the magnificent Snowdon range, Bodnant is for many people the finest garden in Britain. It is, of course, famous for its collections of rhododendrons, camellias and magnolias which in the spring and early summer turn it into a dazzling kaleidoscope of colour, but there are other beauties to enjoy that require little knowledge of plants: the stunning sight of a long tunnel positively cascading with laburnum racemes in early summer, and the Lily Terrace pond, its surface broken up by many rare waterlilies.

The great lily pond is seen at its best between June and September

Bodnant was first established when Henry Pochin planted the conifers in 1875, but it was his daughter, the 1st Lady Aberconway, who extended the gardens to include herbaceous borders and shrubs as well as trees. It was the 2nd Lord Aberconway who gave the 80 acres (32.5ha) of Bodnant to the National Trust in 1949, and it is now the home of his son who was for many years President of the Royal Horticultural Society.

On crossing the front lawn, the eye is immediately captured by the enormous range of colour in the adjoining beds provided by many

different shrubs, among them ceanothus, choisyas, hydrangeas and many clematis, including 'Marcel Moser' and 'Gipsy Queen'. The Rose Terrace offers what is probably the finest views in Bodnant, with the Snowdonia range providing the backdrop to rose beds edged with saxifrages, helianthemums, dwarf campanulas and the soft-textured *Stachys lanata*. Around the walls are rhododendrons, *Mahonia* 'Charity', a row of *Camellia x williamsii* and a splendid pieris with deep red new leaves in April and August.

A flight of steps leading down to the Croquet Terrace brings you to a wisteria-clothed fountain and several lovely shrubs, such as *Eucryphia x nymansensis* 'Nymansay', and numerous viburnums. Continuing downwards, you reach the third terrace with its lily pond and great cedar trees where the buttressed walls provide shelter for magnolias,

buddleias, ceanothus and *Camellia reticulata*, and a hedge of *Erica terminalis* follows the shape of the pond. Four big beds of roses occupy the Lower Rose Terrace, and, on each side, a pergola covered with clematis leads down to the Canal Terrace, its lawns bordered by beds of purple, blue and grey herbaceous plants, by hedges and trees. At one end stands the Pin Mill, an attractive gazebo dating from 1730, and at the other a raised lawn serves as a stage.

Below the canal is the final terrace which boasts a multitude of magnolias, including *Magnolia kobus*, *M. sinensis*, and *M. wilsonii*. The view back towards the house is one of Italian formality – a sharp contrast with the woodland garden dotted with rhododendrons, camellias, azaleas and hydrangeas which clothe the valley right down to the river.

Open daily from March to October. Tel: 0492 650460.

Beds on the Rose Terrace are edged with saxifrages, helianthemums and dwarf campanulas

THE DOROTHY CLIVE GARDEN

Staffordshire

WILLOUGHBRIDGE, 9 MILES (14.5 KM) NORTH-EAST OF MARKET DRAYTON

The cascading waterfall is a distinctive feature of this famous garden

Situated in the splendid rolling countryside on the border between Staffordshire and Shropshire, the Dorothy Clive Gardens were designed and laid out by Colonel Harry Clive as a memorial to his wife. The gardens now cover 7 acres (3ha), but the garden built by the Clives in the 1930s was much smaller. It was when his wife became too infirm to do more than make a circuit of the lawns that Colonel Clive conceived the idea of creating a woodland garden from a 1½ acre (0.5ha) gravel pit, which had been left undisturbed for more than 20 years and consequently was a dense mass of pines, small oaks, silver birches, brambles and holly. Paths were cut through the undergrowth and rhododendrons

planted, and today this magical, enclosed area is a riot of spring colour. Every shade of red, pink, purple, mauve and yellow can be seen, and among the more interesting plants are the blood-red *Rhododendron thompsonii*, rose-pink *R. orbiculare* with its heart-shaped leaves, and the hybrids *R.* 'Sappho' and *R.* 'Goldsworth Yellow'. As the rhododendrons begin to fade, hybrid azaleas, including 'Exbury' and 'Ghent', blossom and fill the air with their heady scent.

After Dorothy Clive's death in 1942, Colonel Clive sold their house, Elds Gorse, and set up a garden trust based at a new bungalow constructed at the entrance to the quarry. He then began to develop the land that sloped down

to the road. A collection of Exbury azaleas were planted, and to celebrate his 80th birthday, his grandchildren planted two blue cedars, *Cedrus atlantica glauca*. Since Colonel Clive's death in 1963 the gardens have been extended, and a rock and scree garden has been a recent addition. Here dwarf tulips and a great many spring bulbs can be seen, while, around the pool, irises and candelabra primulas flourish. In summer, angel's fishing rods show their purplish-red flowers, and ligularias their yellow and orange flowers against green and purple foliage.

Island beds in the lawn contain a wonderful selection of herbaceous plants, shrubs and roses. Along the western edge of the garden is a collection of more than 80 camellias, while heather captures the eye below the striking bark of silver birches.

This garden shows colour at all times of the year. Winter aconites are among the first to appear, followed by crocuses, including *Crocus tommasinianus* with its lavender-coloured flowers. After the rhododendrons are over, the shrub roses provide eye-catching colour, to be followed by gazanias, osteospermums and crocosmias. Dahlias and chrysanthemums begin the autumn season, and, with the elegant pink flowers of the late-flowering *Nerine bowdenii*, the year at Dorothy Clive comes to an end.

Open from April to October, daily. Tel: 0630 81237.

The lower section of the garden, including the lily pond, was designed by John Codrington

DYFFRYN BOTANIC GARDENS
South Glamorgan

ST NICHOLAS, CARDIFF

Far left, a splash of colour in a border, the West Garden

Left, island beds float before the magnificent Palm House

There has been a mansion at Dyffryn, just to the west of Cardiff, since the end of the 16th century but both the present house and the fascinating botanic gardens that surround it date from Edwardian times. John Cory built the house, but it was his third son, Reginald, a well-known figure in horticultural circles, who commissioned Thomas Mawson, the leading landscape architect of his generation, to design the 55 acre (22ha) gardens between 1906 and 1914.

Reginald Cory had a particular interest in the cultivation of dahlias, and also specialised in plants from China and Japan, many of which were introduced to Europe by plant collector E H Wilson for the first time at Dyffryn. Today, much of the fascination of the gardens reflects those early interests, with many impressive Oriental trees and shrubs to be seen, including the two large paper bark maples, *Acer griseum*, and the Chusan palms in the arboretum.

In front of the house is a stunning waterlily canal, surrounded by a great lawn. To the west is a series of 'garden rooms' enclosed by yew hedges, each one with a different theme. There is a Roman Garden, for instance, and a circular Fuchsia Garden which was originally the Rose Garden, plus – a favourite of the Edwardians – an open-air theatre. Beyond, winding walks lead through the informal West Garden, past splendid vistas between colourful beds of herbaceous shrubs and flowers, with magnolias providing a magnificent display in spring and early summer. The Vine Walk is at its best in autumn when the striking foliage colours capture the eye.

Dyffryn prides itself on its glasshouses, the largest of which is the Victorian-style Palm House. Built at the entrance to the gardens in the mid-1960s, it contains few palms now as it is no longer heated, but there is a wonderfully fragrant collection of orange, lemon and grapefruit trees which fill the air with their scent during their flowering season. Near by is a most unusual Chinese rice paper plant, *Aralia papyrifera*, and a large number of showy and brightly coloured camellias.

In the glasshouse range which forms the boundary of the walled Rose Garden is a spectacular collection of tender plants. Here, there are more than 1500 different varieties including succulents from America and Africa and tree-dwelling Bromeliads from the tropical rain forests of South America. Exotic orchids, avocado pears, citrus fruits, rice and cinnamon flourish early in the year in these protected conditions.

Open from March to October, daily.

Bright pelargoniums mix with silvery foliage in front of the house

HODNET HALL
Shropshire

HODNET, 5½ MILES (9 KM) SOUTH-WEST OF MARKET DRAYTON

A section of the mock-Elizabethan buildings can be glimpsed through the lush foliage

Situated in the lovely rolling countryside of mid-Shropshire, Hodnet Hall is surrounded by 60 acres (24ha) of magnificent gardens. The red-brick house was built in 1870 in the later Elizabethan style; below it is a central pool which is the beginning of a chain of lakes running down to the west. These lakes not only create the main axis of the garden, but establish the theme of the garden as a whole.

In 1922, when the pool was little more than a marshy hollow surrounded by elders, laurel and rushes, the present owner's father, Brigadier A G W Heber-Percy, turned what had been his full-time hobby into a gardening career in order to make Hodnet Hall pay its way. In this lime-free environment he created a series of lakes which are thought to be one of the largest water gardens in the country, and filled the grounds

Champagne', 'Mrs A T De-La-Mare', 'The Master' and 'Princess Anne', as well as *Berberis stenophylla* and *Kalmia latifolia*.

The outer ring of the Rose Garden is planted with a collection of old-fashioned roses including 'Comte de Chambord', 'Rose de Resht', 'Felicia' and 'Penelope'. Inside, mixed peonies provide stunning colour around a central bed with a statue, planted with hydrangeas and *Caryopteris x clandonensis* and with old English lavender. Crossing a bridge through the Lower Rose Garden and the Camellia Garden, shining with varieties such as 'Donation' and 'Cornish Snow', you soon find yourself almost absorbed by the giant-

The stream tumbles down a series of giant, mossy steps

with the bright colours of acid-loving plants such as camellias and rhododendrons.

Moving west from the forecourt of the house, you soon come to the entrance to the Woodland Garden with its rhododendrons, specimen trees and spring bulbs that make such an attractive show. Round the side of the private garden is the Broad Walk, which runs along the south front of the house, offering a lovely view over the lake and the surrounding fields to a dovecote built in 1656. Before reaching the Rose Garden you pass the terrace borders, and the slope beyond is planted with Japanese maples, *Acer* 'Dissectum Atropurpureum' and *A. palmatum* 'Palmatifidum', with the rhododendrons 'Tortoiseshell

leaved gunneras of the water garden underplanted with candelabra primulas, irises and great drifts of astilbes.

There is much to see at Hodnet Hall and this is a garden which has been carefully planted to provide colour throughout the year. The daffodils, blossom and bulbs make a brave show in the spring, soon to be followed by rhododendrons, azaleas, lilacs and laburnum. July brings the magnificent roses which contrast with the more vibrant colour of fuchsias, while August is the perfect time for the water plants. The season concludes with the colourful berries and bright foliage of acers, berberis and sorbus.

Open from April to September, on most afternoons. Tel: 0630 84202.

PLAS PENHELIG
Gwynedd

ABERDOVEY

Standing high above the charming harbour of Aberdovey, with spectacular views over the estuary of the River Dyfi to Cardigan Bay, is Plas Penhelig. Today the house is a hotel, but when the estate was established and the 7 acres (2.8ha) of garden laid out in 1908, it was privately owned. Much of the original splendour of the layout has been reclaimed since the present owner,

A view of the house from beyond the hydrangea bed

Mr David Richardson, and his parents, came to Plas Penhelig 10 years ago, and the gardens can once again stand comparison with the most splendid in Wales.

Following the pattern of the original Edwardian garden, you cross the two large lawns in front of the house, framed by herbaceous borders, to reach a large, well-stocked rock garden. The path climbs past a large

bed of hydrangeas, resplendent in their autumnal colours, to the top of the hill, where there is a remarkable collection of mature tree heathers whose perfume in spring is quite overpowering. Beyond, in the woodland, rhododendrons, camellias, azaleas and magnolias make a colourful show in the spring, while a waterfall feeds a large pond whose surface is bright with the subtle pinks, reds and whites of waterlilies.

The path continues to climb past a group of acers, conifers and a Chilean fire bush into a little clearing surrounded by pine trees and heathers. Here, in an especially tranquil setting, is a pets' cemetery, with many small headstones dating back to the early years of this century. Returning in the direction of the house, there is a well-established orchard with some very old apple trees. A gate gives access to a half-acre walled kitchen garden with vines and peaches under glass, which today, just as it did in Edwardian times, supplies the house with vegetables, herbs and fruit.

Plas Penhelig is a garden with spectacular colour to delight the visitor throughout the year, from the blossom and the flowering bulbs in the spring, through the roses, euphorbias and yuccas in the terrace borders in the summer, to the hydrangeas in the autumn.

Open from March to October, on selected afternoons.

A small corn-carrying figure on the Croquet Terrace

THE PRIORY
Hereford and Worcester

KEMERTON, 6 MILES (9.5 KM) SOUTH OF PERSHORE

A short distance to the north-east of Tewkesbury, beneath Bredon Hill, stands The Priory. It is a tranquil, 18th-century house of Cotswold stone, its façade draped with the white trusses of *Solanum jasminoides* and the pink and white bells of *Abelia schumannii in* autumn.

When the Hon. Mrs Elizabeth Healing and her late husband, Peter, came to Kemerton in 1938 it was a dull garden of 3 acres (1ha), without trees, except for some elms on the boundary, and these eventually succumbed to Dutch elm disease. Today, The Priory's layout consists of three outstanding herbaceous borders, a sunken garden with a waterlily pond – surrounded with santolinas and lavender – and a

A delightful composition of pink and white, with the dramatic red border in the background

stream which runs the full length of the property.

The main border, 150ft (45m) long and 20ft (6m) wide, progresses in colour from one end to the other in the manner of Gertrude Jekyll's planting. From grey and variegated foliage at one end, it moves through white, cream, pink and yellow to reach a crescendo of colour and excitement in reds and oranges, before subsiding again to blue and grey. In autumn, *Rosa moyesii* 'Geranium' brings a flash of colour with its orange hips through the mists of more subtle hues.

The theme of the second bed is predominately white and grey, including phloxes, gypsophilla and senecio, with purple sage emphasising the clarity of the primary colour. Although the third border is the smallest, it is, perhaps, the most dramatic. Facing south, its colour scheme is red, and it contains semi-tender plants such as iresines and verbenas as well as *Rosa rubrifolia*, *R.* 'Scarlet Fire', *Berberis purpurifolia* and a purple cotinus. Red cannas, 'Garnet' and 'Firebird' penstemons, and monardas flourish, while love-lies-bleeding and the red dahlia, 'Bishop of Llandaff', are also to be seen.

Mrs Healing has been responsible for the trees at The Priory, planting mulberries, acers and walnuts in the early years, and more recently a *Betula jacquernontii*, with its white bark, a

Autumnal colour in the shady Nut Walk

golden elm, a pocket handkerchief tree and a variegated oak. A pergola, draped with clematis, Dutch honeysuckle, and 'Alberic Barbier' and 'Handel' roses, leads from a 16th-century ruin to the stream garden, with its hostas and bergenias somewhat dwarfed by the abundant gunneras.

Open from June to September, on selected afternoons. Tel: 0386 89258.

STONE HOUSE COTTAGE GARDENS
Hereford and Worcester

STONE, 2 MILES (3 KM) SOUTH-EAST OF KIDDERMINSTER

Below, a herbaceous border in harmonies of mauve, pink, white and silver

Right above, a spectacular raised bed, carefully labelled, stands to one side of the cottage

Right below, the Round Tower, with cream-coloured doves and a rambling rose

The gardens of Stone House Cottage are a plant lover's paradise. In an area covering slightly less than one acre, as many as 2000 plants jostle for space, and the layout of what was originally a kitchen garden has been so carefully devised that a series of separate enclosures and interlocking vistas give the impression that the gardens are bigger than they really are.

When Major and the Hon. Mrs Arbuthnott first came to Stone House Cottage in 1974 the ground had to be completely cleared and, as the southern boundary was not walled, hedges were planted and 'windows' cut into the screen to frame views over the surrounding countryside to the distant but wonderful outline of the Malvern Hills. A bold geometric pattern of intersecting and radiating axes was adopted, and at various points around the enclosure Major Arbuthnott built towers and look-out points to an entertaining design.

On entering the gardens beneath one of these towers, you immediately find yourself in a small courtyard dominated by a water feature which is softened by the dense planting of astilbes, hostas, meconopsis and Solomon's seal. Here there is a choice of three avenues: the left leads under an arch of *Clematis alpina* 'Francis Rivis', interplanted with the climbing rose 'Veilchenblau', through an area rich in shrubs, including the fragrant *Eleagnus augustifolia* 'Caspica', which has yellow flowers in early summer, buddleia, and the lovely *Exochorda x macrantha* 'The Bride'. At the end of

the path are a group of shade-loving plants, including philadelphus and sambucus. A wall draped with honeysuckle, clematis, jasmine and a rose called 'Mermaid' runs towards the house, and pittosporums form strong architectural buttresses to shelter the prolific *Ceanothus* 'Trewithen Blue' as well as winter's bark and a selection of potentillas.

A little further on there is an enclosed garden with an alpine mint bush from Australia sheltering behind surrounding hedges. Around the house there are raised beds containing alpines, penstemons, dianthus, geraniums and thyme. Close by, the herbaceous borders are wonderfully colourful in summer, with salvias, phloxes, tree mallows, agapanthus, sedums and campanulas each holding their own, and the Yellow and White Garden creates a charmingly cool effect. A brick wall running from the house to the entrance is covered with clematis, and among the roses are 'Lady Hillingdon' and 'New Dawn'. Further on there is a great wisteria, and a pergola with a red rose and a pink clematis charmingly intertwined.

Open on selected days. Tel: 0562 69902.

ARLEY HALL GARDENS
Cheshire

NEAR GREAT BUDWORTH, 5 MILES (8 KM) WEST OF KNUTSFORD

Below the clock tower, the Flag Garden features formal beds of lavender and roses

One of the few remaining landed estates in Cheshire, Arley Hall has been owned by the Warburton family since the 12th century, and they built their first house there in 1469. Nothing now remains of that building except the tithe barn, and the present house dates from 1840. The gardens, too, are remarkable, as records show that when Sir Peter and Lady Elizabeth Warburton lived at Arley in the 1740s, they made walled gardens, walks and shubberies. What the visitor sees today is the layout of intimate enclosures mainly established by Rowland and Mary Egerton-Warburton within the earlier brick walls in the 1840s, and now covering 12 acres (5ha).

The gardens are approached along an avenue of pleached limes and entered beneath the 19th-century clock tower. Around the corner of the tithe barn is the Flag Garden, named after

white, but in summer the borders erupt into a kaleidoscope of colour.

Through an archway in the yew hedge are the Tea Cottage and lawns, with beds of shrub and species roses underplanted with geraniums. To the west is the famous Ilex Avenue – clipped holm oaks planted in the 1850s. Near to the avenue is the Fish Garden, set with small conifers and two Japanese cherries; at its end steps lead down to the Sundial Circle, with borders containing the shrub rose 'Erfuhrt' backed by azaleas, kalmias, cistus and philadelphus. The Rootery is now planted with pieris, azaleas and rhododendrons, and in The Rough naturalised bulbs give a bold show in spring. The entrance to the Walled Garden is festooned with honeysuckle, and a lily pond is guarded by four Dawyck beeches.

Turning back towards the Flag Garden you come upon the Herb Garden, which includes mints, thyme, marjorams and bergamots. The Scented Garden is filled with fragrant shrubs and flowers all the year round.

Open from Easter to October, most afternoons. Tel: 0565 777353.

The magnificent double herbaceous borders may be the oldest of their kind in Britain

the flagstones that surround the formal beds of floribunda roses edged by dwarf lavender. The brick walls that enclose it on two sides are covered with honeysuckles, hydrangeas and the flame creeper.

Near by is the Furlong Walk, and as you pass along this elevated terrace you come to a break in the shrub borders which permits entry to Arley Hall's greatest feature, the double herbaceous borders. Perhaps the oldest in the country, for they are shown on a map of 1846, these borders are 90yds long and flank a wide grass path, one side being backed by a brick wall and the other by a yew hedge. Separated by huge buttresses of yew, the plants early in the season are confined to blues, mauves, yellow and

DALEMAIN
Cumbria

DACRE, 3 MILES (5 KM) SOUTH-WEST OF PENRITH

Just to the north of Ullswater, in the magnificent countryside of Cumbria, is Dalemain. The estate seems to have evolved over time in a most natural way, from 12th-century pele tower with its kitchen garden, to an Elizabethan knot garden furnished with herbs. A Stuart terrace dating from 1680 is still to be seen, and, in the 18th century, the building was given a fine new façade, and apple trees such as 'Nonsuch' and 'Keswick Codling' were planted which still bear fruit today. The gardens have been skilfully re-established by the present owners, Mr and Mrs Bryce McCosh, so that a visit to Dalemain is pervaded by that sense of continuity which is so strong an element in good gardening.

The Terrace Walk, with its buttressed retaining wall, is much as it was when Sir Edward Hasell laid it out in the 17th century, although there are now several rambling roses on the wall which invade the gravel path, and a deep herbaceous border below the walls of the house. At the end of the terrace is a handsome Grecian fir with the knot garden in its shadow. Rather reduced in size during the last century, the knot has a marble fountain as its central feature, and consists of symmetrical, low box hedges filled to overflowing with herbs, campanulas and antirrhinums, while the old Victorian Vine Border has the massed seasonal colour of shrub roses, spirea and lilies.

From the knot, the ground slopes upwards to the west, with, on one side of a gravel path, a lawn planted with old apples, plums and pears. On the other side is a deep border with splendid shrub roses edged with sedums, phloxes, rodgersias, meconopsis and irises and, at the top of the garden, a classical summer-house built into an alcove.

A door leads into Lobb's Wood where a path winds between beech and oak trees on the top of a steep bank above the Dacre Beck. Further along the wall is a fine pavilion, with a pointed roof and mullioned windows, dating from 1550. A flight of steep steps leads down to the Wild Garden, started by Mrs McCosh's mother earlier in this century, which is bright with drifts of daffodils in the spring, and with flowering trees and shrubs and the Himalayan blue poppy, *Meconopsis grandis*, in early summer. A visit to Dalemain is a particular pleasure, not only for the sense of historical continuity that it exudes, but for the wonderfully dense vegetation that you can see – undoubtedly a combination of knowledgeable gardening and the climate of Lakeland.

Open from Easter to October, most days. Tel: 0768 486450.

Left, the mysterious doorway to Lobb's Wood

Below, the Terrace Walk, little changed since the 17th century, is a mark of this garden's continuity

HERTERTON HOUSE
Northumberland

HARTINGTON, 2 MILES (3 KM) NORTH OF CAMBO

Herterton House stands high in the uplands of Northumberland. When Frank and Marjorie Lawley came here in 1976 the Tudor house was nearly derelict, and the disused farmyard was littered with broken farm implements and waist-high in stinging nettles. Today, with not a little vision and great gardening skill, all is restored and the gardens are not only delightful and wholly individual, but contain many unusual hardy plants which are also on sale in the adjoining nursery area.

Three separate gardens have been created at Herterton. A small, formal layout fronts on to the road. An evergreen garden in green and gold, it has as its centrepiece a number of topiary features in clipped yew and different varieties of box. Beneath the house wall, which is draped with jasmines, honeysuckles and a fragrant form of *Clematis montana* 'Wilsonii', box-edged beds contain lilies, crown imperials and dicentras.

A gravel path bordered with cream and white 'fumitory' leads into what is now a physic garden laid out as a knot. This charming garden has geometric beds of medicinal herbs, such as tansy, camphor and hyssop, edged with *Saxifraga x urbium* 'Elliott's Variety', while a weeping pear stands in the centre. There are also roses in this enclosure which, together with the honeysuckle that covers the surrounding walls, give off a heady fragrance in full summer.

Behind is the largest of the three enclosures, a walled flower garden. Regular beds separated by gravel paths have been planted in accordance with an overall colour scheme. A collection of old-fashioned daisies is to be seen, with pinks, wallflowers, campions and buttercups, while campanulas, violas, geraniums, avens and Jacob's ladder give the impression of a cottage garden deep in the countryside of the south of England. It says much for the gardening skill of the Lawleys that such beauty can be created 700ft (212m) above sea level in such a windswept environment.

Open from April to October, most afternoons. Tel: 067 074 278.

Far left, bright Oriental poppies catch the eye in this area of the flower garden

Left, honeysuckle against the wall of the loggia fills this corner of the physic garden

LEVENS HALL
Cumbria

5 MILES (8 KM) SOUTH OF KENDAL

The house and dark topiary make a spectacular background for the parterre

Standing at the head of the estuary of the River Kent, close to Kendal, are the amazing gardens of Levens Hall. To most people, Levens is known for its topiary, and the formal layout has a strong flavour of the 17th century. But the garden's links with the adjoining park, now unhappily separated by the A6, show the beginnings of the naturalised gardening movement of the beginning of the 18th century which was to have such a profound influence on the appearance of English gardens and, indeed, of our countryside.

There has been a fortified pele tower on the site of Levens since the 12th century, but the grim medieval building was later turned into a gentleman's residence, and in 1690 Colonel James Grahme began to make it into the finest house in Cumbria, engaging a Monsieur Guillaume Beaumont, who had trained under Le Nôtre at Versailles and worked for King James II at Hampton Court, to lay out the gardens. Today, still immaculately maintained by the owner, Mr C H Bagot, the cones, spirals, pyramids and other geometric shapes in clipped yew and dark green and golden box are still there to be seen, as well as the topiary figures with their own names, such as 'The Judge's Wig' and 'Queen Elizabeth and her Maids of Honour'.

The garden has many ancient, clipped topiary figures

Beneath the great topiary specimens, many of them 20 feet (6m) high, are narrow paths and box-edged beds planted with a riot of seasonal colour – primroses, forget-me-nots, wallflowers, begonias, antirrhinums and geraniums amongst them. Behind the topiary garden a border runs along the walls to the old orchard, and the previous owner, Mr Robin Bagot, planted this with a variety of climbers and shrubs, including clematis, philadelphus, ceanothus and old fruit trees. Beyond the great battlement of the yew hedge is the old orchard, which has flower borders leading to the tall beech hedges, also planted by Beaumont. In summer, soft colours,

particularly blue, line the grassy path, making this an enchanting place. Another grass walk lined with borders leads from the circular beech enclosure to one of the earliest ha-has in the country.

When you cross the A6 you enter the only surviving Elizabethan deer park in the Kendal area. An avenue of splendid oaks planted in the 18th century complements the winding river valley, and you might see the rare Bagot goats and fallow deer. Levens Hall is a magical place, redolent of a period when so many of our modern gardening practices were in their infancy.

Open from Easter to September, most days. Tel: 0539 560321.

A handsome old lead planter, dated 1704

NEWBY HALL

North Yorkshire

4 MILES (6.5 KM) SOUTH-EAST OF RIPON

Newby Hall is set in immaculate parkland on the banks of the River Ure. Built at the end of the 17th century in the manner of Sir Christopher Wren for Sir Edward Blackett, and altered by Robert Adam for William Weddell a century later, Newby is one of the great houses of Yorkshire – a county rich in architectural gems – and its gardens are equally notable. They were designed by Major Edward Compton from 1921 onwards, and since 1977 Robin Compton and his wife, Jane, have restored and replanted the layout, reducing its size in the process from 40 to 25 acres (16 to 10ha).

Although covering a large area, the plan of the garden is based on two main axes. One, the Statue Walk, lies along the south front of the house; and the other, including the main herbaceous borders, runs at right angles from the Lily Pond down to the river. On entering the gardens you soon reach the Statue Walk, its Venetian figures backed by a hedge of red *Prunus pissardii*, and with seats from Italy and from Normandy at either end. Half-way along the Walk, the herbaceous borders sweep down to the river backed by a great yew hedge. A wonderful sight in summer, the flow of the planting is punctuated by viburnums and by red and pink roses, and includes delphiniums, achillea, mallows, campanulas, eryngiums and great clumps of *Cephalaria gigantea*. At the bottom, white roses edged by pale yellow sisyrinchium complete the magnificent display. Returning through the Rhododendron Walk, also densely planted with magnolias and camellias, you pass the sunken Rose Garden enclosed by a copper beech and holly hedge, balanced on the other side of the central borders by the Autumn Garden. This shines with buddleias, hydrangeas and fuchsias, its wattle fencing draped with clematis, roses and honeysuckle.

Just below the Lily Pond is Sylvia's Garden, named after Mrs Compton's mother, which displays a wonderful collection of foliage plants providing year-round interest. The so-called 'Wars of the Roses' Garden features *Rosa gallica* 'officianalis' for Lancaster and *Rosa Alba* 'Semi-plena' for York, with *Rosa mundi* in between. Near by is the Rose Pergola, covered with climbers and ramblers and underplanted with lady's mantle and peonies. This leads down to a fascinating rock garden, incorporating a waterfall and many damp-loving plants, designed by that great gardener, Ellen Willmott, in about 1900. With the striking Lime Avenue and a beautiful Tropical Garden with rodgersias, rheums and magnolias, Newby Hall is undoubtedly one of the most notable gardens to see in the north of England.

Open from April to September, on most days. Tel: 0423 322583.

Left, the great borders sweep down from the house to the river

Below, a scarlet fuchsia breaks up the greenery in this shady corner

BRODICK CASTLE
Strathclyde

ISLE OF ARRAN

Igh above the Firth of Clyde, on the shores of the Isle of Arran, stands Brodick Castle. Backed by the magnificent peak of Goatfell, Brodick occupies a strong defensive position, guarding three routes to western Scotland, and the earliest record of a garden dates from 1710 when a wall was constructed around the present flower garden near to the castle.

However, the layout was over-grown with rhododendrons when the Duchess of Montrose arrived in the 1920s. In her plans to restore and extend the gardens, she was much helped by her son-in-law, Major J P T Boscawen, of Tresco Abbey. Many of the trees and plants came from Tresco, and also from the second generation of plant-hunters like Kingdon-Ward and the great George Forrest who brought back seemingly tender plants from the Himalayas and China which now flourish in the warmth of the Gulf Stream climate of Arran. Today, these magnificent gardens are cared for most skilfully by the National Trust for Scotland.

Left, parts of Brodick are medieval, but the castle was redesigned and rebuilt in the 17th century, and again in 1844

Above, the sundial is surrounded by orderly beds of annuals

Right, a spectacular shower of lilies

Surrounding the castle are spacious lawns edged by colourful beds containing a wide variety of shrubs, including the tall *Eucryphia* 'Nymansay', *Acer* campbellii, olearias and a group of modern hybrid azaleas. A door in the Flower Garden wall leads into a protected enclosure where *Cordyline banksii* and *Ceanothus arboreus* 'Trewithen Blue' flourish, as do acacias, gazanias, fuschias and diascias. In recent years, ribbon-bedding in four long borders has introduced dramatic colour during the summer.

Further down the sloping garden you come to the Pond Garden where plants as diverse in size as gunneras and dwarf primulas thrive. Magnolias and rhododendrons show boldly in spring, while *Crinodendron hookerianum* has pink lantern flowers in summer, and eucryphias and the fragrant lily-of-the-valley tree are at their best in August. The Woodland Garden is planted with rhododendrons and allied shrubs, including many that came from the Isle of Gigha as the gift of the late Sir James Horlick. There are magnolias which produce the most wonderful display of pink flowers on bare branches in April, and a fine *R. sinogrande*. But perhaps the greatest treasure of Brodick is the amazing size of the rhododendron blooms, some of them up to 2ft (0.6m) across.

Open daily. Tel: 0770 2202.

Left, a long view of the castle, across lawns framed with colourful beds

CRARAE GARDENS
Strathclyde

MINARD, 10 MILES (16 KM) SOUTH OF INVERARAY

O n the road that runs along the edge of Loch Fyne, north from Minard Castle towards Inveraray, is the wonderful glen garden of Crarae. Originally started by Grace Campbell in the early years of this century, Crarae was inspired in part by her great nephew, Reginald Farrer – the plant collector and traveller, who introduced into Britain a number of rhododendron species from his trips to Kansu in 1914 and to Upper Burma in 1919 – and perhaps also by Sir John Stirling Maxwell of Pollok. With her son, Sir George Campbell, she spent many years creating this 'Himalayan ravine' garden in a Highland glen. In 1978, Sir George's son, Sir Ilay, transferred the larger part of Crarae to a charitable trust, so that this remarkable garden would be preserved.

These magnificent gardens fill the glen

An unusual find in a country garden – Crarae has its own ancient chambered tomb

Above Crarae is Beinn Ghlas, and where the highest larches end you can see the natural scrub of oak, alder, hazel, birch and rowan that had to be cleared from the lower slopes when the garden was originally created. Beyond the lawns and the two large borders immediately around the Lodge, there are views over Loch Fyne, with, in spring, massed colour of azaleas and a splendid *Acer Tschonoskii*. Following the Crarae Burn further into the Upper Glen the dramatic colours of azaleas, set against a backdrop of decorative hardwoods, catch the eye. The shrub planting includes olearias and the New Zealand pittosporum, which grows strongly.

Close to the waterfall viewpoint there is a fine Japanese dogwood, *Cornus Kousa*, which turns in October to contrast dramatically with the red-leaved azaleas, witch hazel and with *Disanthus cercidifolius*. When you reach the top bridge, azaleas give colour to the foreground, and *Rhododendron davidsonianum* stands beyond with its tulle-like flowers ranging from pale pink to lilac-mauve. Among the hybrid rhododendrons that you can see at Crarae are *Loderi* 'King George', 'Dairymaid', Laura Aberconway' and 'Beauty of Littleworth'. Autumn colour is also quite remarkable, with sorbus, acers, liriodendrons, cotoneasters and berberis competing for attention. With the backdrop of waterfalls and the rushing Crarae Burn, this is indeed a garden of great beauty and individuality.

Open all year, daily. Tel: 0546 86614.

CRATHES CASTLE
Grampian

3 MILES (5 KM) EAST OF BANCHORY

Broad borders almost smother the paths

The first view of Crathes Castle proves that it is all that a Scottish castle should be. The magnificent woodland of Royal Deeside opens up to reveal the romantic tower-house with its turret stairs set in flowing lawns and with eight 'garden rooms', full of colour, contrasting with dark green topiary. It was not until Sir James Burnett and his wife, Sybil, came to Crathes in 1926 that the garden took on its present appearance, and the brilliance of its design and planting is their achievement. Today, the castle and

A path leads from the Rose Garden towards the extravagant topiary

californica and a splendid *Magnolia wilsonii*. To the right is the Golden Garden, with *Viburnum opulus* 'Xanthocarpum', golden berberis, philadelphus, weigela and the rose 'Agnes', and half-way down the White Borders there is a Portugal laurel, *Prunus lusitanica*, from which point the main herbaceous borders run up to the glasshouses. Here, there are syringas, viburnums and an interesting *Dipteronia sinensis*, while the June borders, with the dovecote as a focal point, are planted in the cottage-garden style, with lupins, bearded irises, pyrethrum and several varieties of Oriental poppies.

The Wild Garden is at its best during the autumn with photinias, osmanthus and *Philadelphus wilsonii* contrasting with sorbus and *Liriodendron tulipifera*. In the Upper Pool Garden, Lady Burnett took the colours yellow, red and bronze, and by combining unlikely plants – for instance old roses with heathers or the yellow *Coreopsis vecticillata* with the bronze-leaved form of the wild bugle – she achieved some remarkable effects. The Rose Garden is formally arranged with four triangular beds holding floribunda roses supported by viburnums, a group of crab apples and a pocket handkerchief tree. Clearly inspired both by Gertrude Jekyll and by Lawrence Johnston at Hidcote, the gardens at Crathes Castle hold many treasures for the plant lover and the garden visitor alike.

Open daily. Tel: 033 044 651.

gardens are under the care of the National Trust for Scotland.

Entering the gardens brings you directly into the White Borders. Beyond the West Border, with its herbaceous plants of blue and pink, steps lead to the Aviary Border, which shows olearias, clematis, *Carpentaria*

The road east from Forfar follows the valley of the Lunan Water. Near to Guthrie is the House of Pitmuies, one of the loveliest estates in this part of Scotland, already rich in such properties. The harled three-storeyed mansion was rebuilt in 1730 by Mr Ogilvy, and 50 years later records show that the walled garden was in existence. The foundations of the modern garden are most probably Victorian, but the beauty and immaculate condition of the layout today is due to the late Mr Farquhar Ogilvie and his wife, Margaret.

Entering the gardens from the car park, you come first to the kitchen garden, which, in traditional fashion, still provides vegetables, fruit and flowers for the house. Beyond, an archway of weeping pears introduces the central walk of the summer borders, flanked by hedges of red cherries and beds planted with soft-coloured summer flowers. Below the house, and linked by stone steps, are three gardens of great beauty and variety. Around a central fountain, with tall bulrushes and waterlilies, ferns, alpines and mallows grow among the paving, while, on one side of the garden are exquisite old-fashioned roses and long beds of massed delphiniums, including some

HOUSE OF PITMUIES
Tayside

GUTHRIE, 8 MILES (13 KM) EAST OF FORFAR

varieties which have been at Pitmuies for more than 70 years. A rambling-rose hedge separates the Rose Garden from the yellow and blue borders which lead back to the house.

Along the Trellis Walk, clematis and climbing roses contrast with blue Himalayan poppies, and ferns, hostas and bergenias flourish close to a row of Tibetan cherry trees. Pinks and violas brighten the paved area and, in raised beds, there is a collection of old and modern cinquefoils. In the Alpine Meadow, which was once the drying ground for the 18th-century 'Gothick' wash-house, autumn mowing encourages a marvellous display of snowdrops and crocuses in spring. By early summer shrub roses and penstemons border the terrace walk which leads to the Turbie Burn. Between the Burn and the Vinny Water, beeches and limes shade the walk, overlooked by an extraordinary turreted dovecote which bears the date 1643 and the Ogilvy and Guthrie arms. The Vinny Garden has some variegated hollies, a monkey puzzle and a paperbark maple, while the walk down to the Black Loch takes you through woodland interplanted with rhododendrons and azaleas.

Open from April to October, daily. Tel: 024 12 245.

Magnificent, densely packed flower borders are flanked by hedges of red cherry

PLANTS FROM THE PAST
East Lothian

BELHAVEN, DUNBAR

Within a mile of the North Sea coast in Scotland is one of the more remarkable country gardens, Plants from the Past, situated in North Street, Belhaven. During the past five years, Dr David Stuart and James Sutherland have restored a walled kitchen garden and replanted it to a mid-18th-century design, so that, to turn from the narrow village streets through the gates and into a fine parterre is like taking a step back in time. The plant conservationist will also be delighted, however, as the two owners are not interested in modern cultivars, but rather in older forms of herbaceous plants.

Totally derelict when it was found, the site is surrounded by lovely sandstone walls and slopes gently towards the beach. On the higher ground, the owners found an early 18th-century building that seemed to have been used as an apple store, and boasted a tiny fireplace in the upstairs room, and this charming structure, now restored, serves as the office. From the upper windows, the parterre, which follows that planted at Yester House in the 1750s, seems to consist of a maze of gravel paths separating colourful beds, while at one side of the layout a raised grass walkway leads through to the nursery.

With a determined effort to recreate the planting of the correct date, the owners have placed mandrakes next to the lovely *Primula vulgaris subsp. Sibthorpii*, and 'Giant White' lavender alongside *Artemisia pontica*. Above these plants are Persian lilac, *Eleagnus augustifolia* and many old roses from 'Pompon de Bourgogne' to 'Maiden's Blush' and 'Quatre Saisons'.

Herbs, too, are historically accurate, with a cornel bush and a myrobalan, as well as sorrels, tarragon and tree onions. Plymouth strawberries, their seeds on the surface of the fruit turned into little points, are to be found, together with flamed pinks, double buttercups and soapworts, a pretty double form of the greater celandine, and tulips that range from 'Keizerskroon' to *Tulipa clusiana*. At Plants from the Past, the visitor can enjoy the dramatic colours, subtle textures and the half-remembered scents of old varieties secure in the knowledge that each purchase they make will help preserve the future for some of these rare plants.

Open from March to September, most days. Tel: 0368 63223.

Left and below, Plants from the Past cultivates a splendid collection of older varieties

INDEX